Brahms —
Chissel
Gt. Composers

Brahms

Other books in this series

BACH *Imogen Holst*
BEETHOVEN *Stanley Sadie*
BRITTEN *Imogen Holst*
BYRD *Imogen Holst*
CHOPIN *Joan Chissell*
DELIUS *Eric Fenby*
HANDEL *Stanley Sadie*
HAYDN *H. C. Robbins Landon*
HOLST *Imogen Holst*
LISZT *Alan Walker*
MENDELSSOHN *Michael Hurd*
ROSSINI *James Harding*
SCHUMANN *Alan Walker*
VAUGHAN WILLIAMS *Michael Hurd*
WAGNER *Elaine Padmore*

The Great Composers

Brahms

Joan Chissell

FABER AND FABER   3 QUEEN SQUARE   LONDON

To F.H. in grateful memory

First published in 1977
by Faber and Faber Limited
3 Queen Square London WC1
Printed in Great Britain by
the University Printing House, Cambridge

All rights reserved
ISBN 0 571 10791 5
© Joan Chissell 1977

Contents

I	Young Days in Hamburg	page 9
II	First Travels	17
III	Heart-ache	28
IV	Picking up the threads	37
V	The Lure of Vienna	47
VI	On the Crest of the Wave	61
VII	Conquests and Conflicts	71
VIII	Approaching the End	89
	Suggestions for Further Reading	98
	Summary of Brahms's Works	99
	Index	101

Illustrations

The house where Brahms was born	*page* 8
Brahms's tin soldiers	11
Brahms and Eduard Reményi, 1853	15
Robert and Clara Schumann, after a daguerreotype taken in Hamburg in 1850	15
Brahms at twenty. Drawing by J. B. Laurens	16
Joseph Joachim, 1853. Drawing by J. B. Laurens	21
Brahms approaching thirty	21
Brahms's first letter to Breitkopf & Härtel, 8 November 1853	27
A page from the manuscript of Brahms's Variations on a Theme by Schumann, Op. 9 (1854)	30
Brahms at the piano, 1856	33
Brahms's father, Jakob, 1838	36
Brahms's mother, Christiane, in later life	36
Brahms's sister, Elise, 1860	36
Brahms's brother, Fritz, 1870	36
Brahms's lodgings at Hamm	39
A page from the manuscript of 'Wiegenlied', Op. 49, No. 4	40
Agathe von Siebold	44
Brahms in 1870	53
Theodor Billroth	55
Brahms, Johann Strauss and Hans Richter	62
Eduard Hanslick	63
Elisabeth von Herzogenberg	69
The house where Brahms stayed near Thun	78
The house where Brahms stayed in Ischl	82
The mature celebrity	83
Brahms on his way to 'The Red Hedgehog'. Silhouette by Otto Böhler	85

Illustrations

Brahms in 1893	85
Brahms at Gmunden with the daughters of a friend	86
Brahms with Johann Strauss in Ischl	87
Brahms and the Beggar	89
Brahms at Ischl in 1896	92
Brahms at the wedding anniversary of his friends, the Fellingers, 1896	93
Johannes Brahms's signature	97

Music Examples

1	Hungarian Dance No. 5	page 16
2	Scherzo in E flat minor for piano, Op. 4	19
3	Andante from Piano Sonata in C, Op. 1	24
4	Joachim's FAE motto; Brahms's FAF motto	25
5	Adagio from Piano Concerto in D minor, Op. 15	35
6	'Wiegenlied', Op. 49, No. 4	41
7	German Requiem, Op. 45, second movement	50–51
8	Waltz in E major for piano from Op. 39, (originally for piano duet)	56
9	String Sextet in G major, Op. 36, first movement	58
10	Symphony in C minor, Op. 68, finale (horn theme)	63
11	Symphony in C minor, finale (main theme)	64
12	Symphony in D major, Op. 73, first movement	65
13	Adagio from the Violin Concerto, Op. 77	67
14	Symphony in F major, Op. 90, first movement	73
15	Symphony in E minor, Op. 98, opening theme of the finale based on a theme borrowed from Bach. (a) Bach, (b) Brahms	74
16	Symphony in E minor, finale	75
17	Violin Sonata in G, Op. 78, finale	76–7
18	'Regenlied', Op. 59, No. 3	77
19	Intermezzo in E flat major for piano, Op. 117, No. 2	91
20	'O Welt, ich muss dich lassen', No. 11 from Eleven Chorale Preludes for organ, Op. 122	94–5

Young Days in Hamburg I

'He had only been living with us for a week when he wanted me to become his wife. I could hardly believe it, because our ages were so different.' This was how Brahms's mother, Christiane, subsequently described her marriage in 1830, at forty-one, to the twenty-four-year-old Jakob Brahms, newly arrived as lodger in the house of the sister and brother-in-law with whom Christiane herself lived in Hamburg. Christiane was a small, frail seamstress with a slight limp, and she helped in her sister's hardware shop as well as earning what she could with her needle. Jakob was an unexceptional double-bass player, who, determined to make music his career rather than follow in the footsteps of his innkeeper father at Heide, had run away to apprentice himself to one or two not too distant town musicians before setting out at nineteen to try his luck in Hamburg. In time he found a place in the sextet that performed in the fashionable pleasure gardens of the Alster Pavilion, and even in the municipal theatre and Philharmonic Orchestra. But it was a hand-to-mouth existence at first, ranging from horn playing in the militia band to casual jobs with his flute or any other instrument he could tackle in sailors' taverns and dance-halls. Small wonder that his neat new lodgings and the sympathetic attentions of Christiane so quickly sharpened his desire for a home of his own.

    Nothing could have been more dark and squalid than No. 60 Speckstrasse (as it is now called), not far from Hamburg's docks, where on the first floor they rented a cramped, three-roomed apartment. But Christiane, of slightly better stock than her husband, at once tried to brighten it with pot-plants and caged birds on the window-sills. More important still, in view of her age, she lost no time in giving Jakob three children, Elise (born in 1831), Fritz (born in 1835), and mid-way between them, on 7 May 1833, Johannes. Despite worries caused by a few of Jakob's

The House in Hamburg where Brahms was born

attempted short-cuts to prosperity, including breeding chickens, pigeons and rabbits, Christiane's gift for home-making created a strong family bond. She loved celebrating birthdays, for which as an excellent cook she would make a special egg-nog; also other landmarks in the calendar like Christmas, when there was always a goose. As time went on and Jakob's usefulness as an all-rounder became better known, they even managed to afford better apartments.

On one point Jakob and Christiane were firmly agreed: no effort must be spared to give the boys a good education. So after five years at a small private school, Johannes moved on at eleven to a more progressive grammar school, its curriculum including English and French as well as Latin, and gymnastics (with modern apparatus) as well as thorough Bible study. English always gave him trouble, French not so much, despite his execrable accent. He only played truant once and always regretted it since it earned him a severe hiding from his father. Perhaps the school's greatest service was in awakening his literary interests. When he left at fifteen he had already started to call himself Johannes Kreisler, junior, after the eccentric musician of E. T. A. Hoffmann's novel, *Kater Murr*, and he liked to copy extracts from his favourite authors and poets into note-books which he called 'Young Kreisler's Treasure' ('Schatzkästlein des jungen Kreisler'). He also began to collect a small library of his own — largely bought from Hamburg's second-hand book-stalls — which he treasured as much as his tin soldiers.

But nothing fired his imagination more than his father's world of music. By six he had worked out his own system of lines and dots for writing down tunes. As he subsequently put it, 'I invented a system of notation before I knew that one had already long been in existence!' At seven, tired of experimenting with his father's instruments, he demanded to learn the piano. Here Jakob could not help. So with a percipience remarkable in a happy-go-lucky thirty-one-year-old, he took his son to visit Friedrich Wilhelm Cossel. No younger piano teacher in Hamburg was sounder, for although Cossel had not made the grade as a soloist, he had studied with the enlightened Eduard Marxsen of Altona, and was far more drawn to pupils with talent than money. The young Johannes, with long fair hair and serious blue eyes, immediately interested him. Cossel's only worry was when Johannes sometimes neglected studies by Czerny, Clementi, Cramer and other finger-strengtheners of the day if the urge came to write pieces of his own. All the same, such progress had been made by 1843 that Jakob decided to present Johannes in a 'benefit' concert. Besides joining his father and various colleagues in a piano quartet by Mozart and Beethoven's quintet for piano and wind, Op.16, Johannes played a virtuoso piece by Herz so brilliantly that an American impresario who chanced to be there proposed a tour of America on the spot. Jakob could scarcely restrain his delight. Cossel, when told, was horrified. For a long time he had felt the need of Marxsen's mature help in guiding youthful talent so remarkable: now he begged his old master to intervene to prevent this threatened commercial exploitation. Reason won the day. For another year or so, on Marxsen's insistence, Johannes had regular lessons from both teachers. Eventually it was unanimously agreed that Marxsen should assume full control – which he was now fully prepared to do without payment.

Like Cossel, Marxsen put Johannes's piano-playing first, notably strengthening his left hand to permit sturdy independence in cross-rhythms. But Marxsen was a great believer in general musicianship. He encouraged Johannes to transpose at the keyboard. Rudiments of music, harmony and counterpoint all came in for their fair share of attention, and as an indefatigable composer himself, he was far more interested than Cossel had been in his young pupil's free composition. As he later remarked, 'though his first attempts produced nothing of consequence, I

perceived in them a mind in which, as I was convinced, an exceptional and deeply original talent lay dormant'. Marxsen himself had studied composition in Vienna with Ignaz von Seyfried, who in childhood had taken piano lessons from Mozart, besides enjoying the acquaintanceship of Haydn and Beethoven. Marxsen's piano teacher, Carl Maria von Bocklet, also had links with Beethoven as well as being a close friend of Schubert. These legendary figures of the recent past, rather than the rising generation of romantic explorers, were Marxsen's heroes. Revering his teacher, Johannes warmed to the challenge of the great classical tradition, with its emphasis on argument rather than sensation, design rather than colour, discipline rather than unbridled emotionalism. He showed little interest in the intimate 'character' piece beloved by Schumann and Chopin; still less in the popular virtuoso-variation style.

Trying not to disappoint Marxsen, on top of school work and constant readiness to augment the meagre family income by taking on odd jobs in tavern bands at night, proved a strain. As he approached his fourteenth birthday, Johannes was anaemic and pale. But his father, already deputizing at the Alster Pavilion, had the good fortune to strike up an acquaintance with one of its regular patrons called Adolph Giesemann; the owner of a small paper-mill at the country town of Winsen on the Luhe, he loved music and played the guitar himself. On hearing of Jakob's worries about his son's health, he was only too pleased to invite Johannes to stay for the summer, the more so since his own thirteen-year-old daughter, Lieschen, badly needed encouragement with her own piano playing. The visit was enough of a success to be repeated in 1848. For Johannes they remained the two most cherished memories of his childhood. After the streets of Hamburg it was a revelation to wander off into the woods and fields for whole days on end, aware of creative stirrings never experienced before. With Lieschen as companion, he would look for birds' nests, gather wild flowers, swim in the river, fish in the pond, or watch the animals kept by his hosts before returning to enjoy Frau Giesemann's wholesome country cooking and fresh milk, find some good books to share (Tieck's *Magelone* was one of their favourites, and Brahms recalled it many years later by setting its lyrics as a song-cycle), or settle down at the piano. Though Lieschen took her own music none too seriously, Johannes could not relax: each week he had to return to Hamburg for his lesson with Marxsen. Sometimes Lieschen would accompany him on these journeys, which most of all they liked to make by steamer. Lieschen's uncle, in charge of the refreshment department at Winsen railway station and on the steamers, was able to arrange this for them, and in Hamburg Lieschen could always share Elise's room at Brahms's home. During 1848, Lieschen's father bought them gallery tickets for the Hamburg Opera, once to hear Mozart's *The Marriage of Figaro*, the next time Kreutzer's *Das Nachtlager von Granada* (The Night-camp of Granada), then enjoying a great vogue.

Winsen itself brought its musical excitements too. Though the Men's Choral Society consisted of only a dozen or so local schoolmasters and tradesmen, they were keen enough to hold practices every Saturday, either in the main school or the best inn, the Deutsches Haus, both of which had pianos. Hearing about the Giesemanns' young musical guest, they lost little time in inviting him to accompany or conduct them. The school children also begged his help in choosing and preparing a serenade to sing for their headmaster's birthday. Co-operating with the Men's Choir gave Johannes particular pleasure, so much so that he composed two part-songs for them in 1847, and the following year made two special arrangements of the folk-songs they so much liked to sing. This was his first close encounter with his country's great heritage of national song: its lure was strong enough for him to continue to collect folk-songs, and arrange them for various solo voices or choral groups, throughout most of his life. Parting from everyone at the end of the 1848 holiday was particularly sad. He even wrote a farewell poem starting, 'Farewell, farewell, ye friends upright and simple', to recite to his faithful choir at their last practice.

Schooldays were now over. When Brahms returned to Hamburg he was fifteen. It was time to start earning his living. Since his piano playing had caught the attention of that American impresario a few years back, it was on the piano that he pinned his hope. With a few local instrumentalists and singers to share responsibilities, he made two platform appearances that first winter and spring. Knowing he would have to show off his technique in the bravura display the general public then loved so much, at the first concert in September 1848, he included Döhler's 'Fantasia on Themes from Rossini's *Tell*', and at the second in April 1849, Thalberg's 'Fantasia on Themes from *Don Juan*' besides a 'Fantasia for Piano on a favourite Waltz' of his own. But he was determined that everyone should know that this was not where his heart really lay: significantly a prelude and fugue by Bach found a place in the first programme, and more daringly still, he chose Beethoven's 'Waldstein' Sonata to open the second. Public response was good, and passing newspaper comment kind. Invitations followed to contribute solos to several other miscellaneous programmes given by Hamburg musicians. But he was now too old to rouse interest as a child prodigy, too young to compete with Hamburg's many famous international visitors. For a regular source of income, paltry as it was, he was thrown back on giving piano lessons, accompanying at the State Theatre, or most irksome of all, playing in the same old taverns where his father had earned his first money. Hamburg was a busy port. Sailors on shore-leave had little thought for anything but drink and sex. The basic facts of life were brought home to him crudely at an impressionable age. But a book of poems propped up on the music stand brought some relief: in imagination, at least, he could escape from the smoke, the noise, the squalor.

With nothing in sight but this dreary routine, he was overjoyed one day to receive a commission from the publisher, Cranz, to make arrangements of popular tunes for bands or pleasure-garden ensembles, and also to compose some salon music of his own. Never before had money been so agreeably earned: even as a practical test of skill, after long hours of study, it was a challenge he found irresistible. He took the precaution of sheltering under pseudonyms. But in later life he was always far more proud than ashamed if he ever came across any of this youthful hack-work. Even at the time hardship never made him bitter, for he had a rich inner world of his own, nourished by literature, in which to take refuge. As he told a friend, 'the best songs came into my head while brushing my boots before dawn'. His susceptibility to romantic verse was then keen enough for a mere, slow reading-through of a poem to bring a melody spontaneously to mind. Nor was he only preoccupied with songs. Powerful ideas for big piano works began to course through his head in his later teens.

By this time his younger brother, Fritz, was showing unmistakable leanings towards a musical career too. But no deep sympathy developed between them. Without exceptional talent, Fritz adopted a more careless attitude to life, not untinged with jealousy when people sometimes referred to him as 'the wrong Brahms'. For friendship Johannes still turned a great deal towards the Giesemanns and their musical circle in Winsen. He also made quite a few stimulating new contacts in Hamburg, including a young music student, Louise Japha, whose enthusiasm for Robert and Clara Schumann, when they visited Hamburg in 1850, prompted Brahms to leave a packet of his own manuscripts at their hotel – which the Schumanns, rushed off their feet, were

Brahms and Eduard Reményi, 1853   *Robert and Clara Schumann, 1850*

compelled to return unopened. One night when engaged as accompanist at a music party given by a rich Hamburg merchant, Brahms also met a mercurial Hungarian-Jewish violinist, only three years his senior, called Eduard Reményi, whose revolutionary activities during the 1848 uprisings compelled him to seek refuge wherever he could. His temperamental interpretations of Hungarian gypsy music captivated Brahms enough for them to play together as much as possible until the police caught up with Reményi and he had to flee to America. Late in 1852, however, he was back in Hamburg, and in the spring of 1853 asked Brahms to join him as accompanist on a concert tour of not too distant towns where they had contacts. Being ambitious, Reményi also hoped that *en route* they might solicit the attention of one or two really influential musicians like Joachim, whom he had known as a student in Vienna. Brahms, now twenty, was glad of even the briefest prospect of escape. Little did he guess it was a journey which was to change the whole course of his life.

1 Hungarian Dance No. 5, originally for piano duet.

Brahms at twenty

First Travels   II

Not surprisingly it was for Winsen, place of happy memories, that they set out on 19 April 1853. Their first concert was scheduled for the end of the month at the Rusteberg club-house, and with an invitation to stay with the Giesemanns as long as they liked, they had ample opportunity for rehearsing the programme chosen for the whole tour. Beethoven's C minor Sonata, Op. 30, and Vieuxtemps's Concerto in E were the main works, besides Ernst's *Élégie* and groups of violin solos that gave Reményi ample opportunity to show off, especially Hungarian dances. As Brahms had so many friends in the neighbourhood the hall was well-filled, bringing them profits sufficient to carry them on to Celle. But out of consideration for a sick schoolmaster member of the Winsen Men's Choir, they went over to Hoopte to repeat the programme in his schoolroom before leaving.

Thanks to friends of the Giesemanns, even in Celle they did not arrive as strangers. This concert, arranged for 2 May in the Wierss'schen Room, made quite a stir because of the low-pitched piano. Rather than ask Reményi to tune down his violin, Brahms transposed the whole programme, which he always played from memory, into keys a semitone higher than written. The feat even impressed Reményi enough for him to tell the audience what Brahms was doing. Moving on to Lüneberg, their good audience at Herr Balcke's Hall on 9 May was more or less guaranteed by the son and daughter-in-law of one of Brahms's most loyal supporters in Winsen (the local administrator, Herr Blume) who gave a private party in advance to introduce the young visitors to the neighbourhood. By general demand this concert had to be repeated the following day, after which Reményi and Brahms returned to Celle for a requested second appearance there, too. Some biographers suggest they then chanced their luck in Hildesheim, on far slenderer contacts, with results that only paid off after nocturnal serenading (emboldened by drink) of the town's leading patroness of the arts. But there are no newspaper advertisements or reports to prove it.

Reményi now considered the moment ripe to look up his old compatriot and fellow-student Joachim who, although well launched on a solo career, was only twenty-two, and still glad to have the job of Kapellmeister to the King of Hanover as anchorage. So it was to Hanover that Reményi and Brahms now made their way, arriving about the middle of May. The visit was a total surprise to Joachim, and naturally it was with his ebullient fellow-countryman that easy relations were established first. Brahms was shy and silent. He had never forgotten Joachim's performance of Beethoven's Violin Concerto in Hamburg five years before and, although only two years Joachim's junior, felt a mere mortal in the presence of a god. But soon tiring of Reményi's flamboyance, Joachim found himself increasingly drawn to his unknown visitor with the serious blue eyes and curiously high-pitched voice, especially on learning that he was not only a pianist but wrote music too.

When Brahms played movements from two recently completed Sonatas in F sharp minor and C major, a turbulent Scherzo in E flat minor written as early as 1851, and a song, 'Liebestreu', Joachim was spell-bound by the music's 'undreamt-of originality and power', as he subsequently put it, and equally by Brahms's playing, which he found 'tender and imaginative, free and fiery', and his 'inspired' appearance at the keyboard. The visit came to an abrupt end when the police heard that the two travellers, one of them a wanted revolutionary, had presumed to play to the King. But they left with an introduction to Liszt at Weimar and, for Brahms, an open invitation to return to Joachim's home if he should ever find himself in need.

Liszt, now in his early forties, had withdrawn from the concert platform. With the intellectual Princess Caroline von Sayn-Wittgenstein at his side, he was living in style on the Altenburg as self-appointed leader of the 'New German' progressive school, surrounded by a considerable number of young friends and colleagues. Any artist was assured of a welcome provided he came as a disciple. Reményi could scarcely wait to pay court to so illustrious a compatriot, eventually presenting himself and his accompanist in early June.

With new music his main interest, naturally Liszt's immediate concern, after Joachim's eulogies, was to satisfy his curiosity about Brahms. Summoned to the house, Brahms was horrified to find not only

2 Scherzo in E flat minor, Op. 4.
The earliest piano composition Brahms allowed into print, composed at the age of 18.

First Travels

Liszt awaiting him, but a room full of pupils and associates too – including Germans as gifted as Raff and Peter Cornelius, as well as William Mason from far away New York. Overawed by the sophistication of it all, Brahms lost confidence. He felt a provincial from Hamburg again. Nothing would induce him to play. Liszt's reaction was to pick up the manuscript of the E flat minor Scherzo and sight-read it with an assurance that took Brahms's breath away, meanwhile keeping up a critical commentary on the music that suggested he was by no means unimpressed. Less constrained interchanges in the next few weeks confirmed Liszt's interest. But nothing could disguise the fact that there was no close bond of sympathy between them.

Only Liszt's piano playing really roused Brahms's own enthusiasm: the music itself, particularly the B minor Piano Sonata, seemed to him to wear its heart on its sleeve. Granted a few more years, he might have better appreciated the intellectual vitality underpinning Liszt's love of display. As it was, he lacked the courtier-like art of paying lip-service, which sufficiently incensed Reményi, totally enslaved by Weimar, for him to tell Brahms that their association was at an end. Brahms was as surprised as he was troubled. There seemed no alternative but to return to Hamburg, admit failure, and face parental disappointment. Then he suddenly remembered Joachim's invitation. A desperate letter to Göttingen, where Joachim was attending a summer lecture course at the University in history and philosophy, brought the warm-hearted reply, 'Come'.

July in Göttingen was heaven. As Joachim liked to compose, too, they regularly criticized each other's works, with such profitable results that for several years they continued to send each other contrapuntal exercises by post – any failure to fulfil the required task involved the culprit in the payment of a mutually agreed fine. Though Brahms preferred not to attend the lecture course, he revelled in every other aspect of student life, the eating and drinking, the outings, the parties. Before long his mother, who had promised to write him a letter each week he was away, grew worried:

> How can you live away from home without money? If you have to get every little thing from Joachim, you will be under too great an obligation to the gentleman. You had better write to Herr Marxsen. He can advise you in everything. But you must write the exact truth, otherwise the same thing will happen as with Reményi. You understand people too little and trust them too much.

Joseph Joachim, 1853 *Brahms approaching thirty*

Joachim's response was immediate. To Frau Brahms he wrote a long, personal letter including these words:

> Your Johannes has stimulated my work as an artist to an extent beyond my hopes . . . his purity, his independence, young though he is, and the singular wealth of his heart and intellect find sympathetic utterance in his music, just as his whole nature will bring joy to all who come into spiritual contact with him. . . . I can only hope that our new bond will find the blessing of your approval.'

Excitement at such words from one of Joachim's stature bubbled over from Hamburg to Winsen. As Elise Brahms read the letter to the Giesemanns, Lieschen wrote it down to show to all their friends. But perhaps just a little disturbed by his mother's words, Brahms grew reluctant to impose on his warm-hearted friend any longer. He also began to feel a great need, such as was so often to come to him in later life, to go off into the country to sort out his thoughts, personal and musical. With characteristic generosity Joachim proposed a recital together to raise funds, and in mid-August Brahms set off alone, staff in hand and ruck-sack on his back, for a walking tour of the Rhineland.

This time his mother fretted about physical danger:

> Such steep rocks! How easily you could fall there! I tremble when I think of it. Your chest is strong, of course, but one can overdo things with so much climbing. . . . Therefore Johannes dear, please take care of yourself and for heaven's sake don't go out in a thunderstorm.

But Brahms himself was on top of the world, as he revealed when writing to salute his good Winsen friend, Herr Blume, on his golden wedding in September 1853:

> I have passed a heavenly summer, such as I have never before known. After spending some gloriously inspiring weeks with Joachim at Göttingen, I have now been rambling about for five weeks according to heart's desire, on the divine Rhine. I hope to be able to pass this winter at Hanover in order to be near Joachim, who is equally noble as man and artist.

His happiness was enhanced by one or two introductions given him by Joachim. J. W. Wasielewski, Music Director at Bonn, invited him to stay for several days, so did the Deichmann family at Mehlem. His visit to these influential Mehlem patrons of the arts was particularly memorable, not just because they had young sons to accompany him on expeditions, but because of their enthusiasm for Schumann. Friends like Louise Japha and Joachim had always told him that Schumann was a composer after his own heart – had he not written a big piano work called *Kreisleriana*, inspired by Brahms's own beloved E. T. A. Hoffman hero? Now, exploring a vast amount of Schumann's music at Mehlem, Brahms gradually recognized a fellow romantic who also valued the same classical principles he himself had been taught to revere. At last he decided to swallow his pride about those manuscripts Schumann had returned unopened in 1850 and do what Joachim had so ardently pressed him to do. After visiting Carl Reinicke and Ferdinand Hiller in Cologne, he boarded a train for Düsseldorf, and at the end of September knocked on the Schumanns' door.

Schumann by now was forty-three, and Clara his wife, just thirty-four. Ideally happy as they were with their six children, Schumann's increasing bad health was making it difficult for him to discharge his

First Travels

duties adequately as the city's Director of Music, and was driving him into a dangerously introspective world of his own, with sinister leanings towards the occult. Joachim's performance of Beethoven's Violin Concerto at the Lower Rhine Festival that spring, leading to a warm personal friendship, had been the greatest tonic in his life for years: any Joachim protegé arriving just then would have been assured of a welcome.

Immediately he went inside, Brahms felt at home. Here, there was none of the sophistication that had over-awed him so much at the Altenburg. Warmed by a simple greeting, and as relaxed as he was happy, he first played his C major Sonata to Robert and Clara, then in the course of the next few days, everything else he had written, including a Fantasy Trio for piano, violin and cello, a Sonata for violin and piano, and several new songs. Both Robert and Clara were overwhelmed. As Clara put it in her diary:

> He played us sonatas, scherzos etc. of his own, all of them showing exuberant imagination, depth of feeling, and mastery of form. Robert says that there was nothing that he could tell him to take away or to add. It is really moving to see him sitting at the piano, with his interesting young face, which becomes transfigured when he plays, his beautiful hands, which overcome the greatest dificulties with perfect ease (his things are very difficult), and in addition these remarkable compositions. He has studied with Marxsen in Hamburg, but what he played to us is so masterly that one cannot but think that the good God sent him into the world ready-made. He has a great future before him, for he will first find the true field for his genius when he begins to write for the orchestra. Robert says there is nothing to wish except that heaven may preserve his health. . . .

There was no question of Brahms being allowed to leave. With their own large family, the Schumanns could not put him up. But from modest lodgings nearby he was a constant guest for meals and at their frequent musical parties, for they wanted the whole neighbourhood to make the acquaintance of 'he who was bound to come', as Schumann wrote enthusiastically to Joachim of his friend. Meeting up again with his Hamburg friend, Louise Japha, and her sister, now living in Düsseldorf, gave Brahms great pleasure. But there were painters and writers, including Bettina von Arnim and her daughter Gisela, besides musicians in the circle into which he found himself suddenly plunged. Often

First Travels

he was invited to join them on excursions into the country as well as to make music in their homes.

After the grim urgency of wage-earning in Hamburg even before leaving school, this sudden realization that life was something to be lived and enjoyed made him as young in heart again as he had been with Joachim in Göttingen. Once, on a trip to the Grafenburg, he ran into a field and impulsively pulled up turnips which, after careful cleaning, he teasingly offered to the ladies for refreshment. Nothing tired him. Everyone loved him for his unaffected exuberance when elated, even while recognizing that his simple upbringing had not included the ultimate in finesse, such as considering other people's feelings when expressing opinions.

One of his closest confidants at this time was Schumann's twenty-two-year-old pupil, Albert Dietrich. Secretive as he usually was about what lay behind his music, Brahms confessed to Dietrich how often themes came to him when he recalled the words of folk-songs, such as the slow movement of the F sharp minor Sonata sparked off by 'Mir ist

First Travels

leide, dass der Winter beide, Wald und auch die Heide, hat gemachet kahl' ('Woe is me that winter has made both wood and heath bare') and the central episode of the finale of the C major Sonata, suggested by the Scottish song, 'My heart's in the Highlands'. For the Andante of his C major Sonata he borrowed the tune of the old Minnelied, 'Verstohlen geht der Mond auf' ('The moon steals up') as a theme for variations, writing the words into the score. When his third Sonata in F minor, occupying him all that summer and autumn, eventually appeared, its Andante had a verse from Sternau at its head: 'Der Abend dämmert, das Mondlicht scheint, Da sind zwei Herzen in Liebe vereint, und halten sich selig umfangen' ('Evening falls, and in the light of the rising moon two loving hearts fuse in rapture'). But this richly romantic movement (whose main theme returns poignantly transformed by minor tonality in the fourth movement, subtitled 'Rückblick') owes more to the sentiment of the poem than to mere verbal rhythm: it was the last time Brahms ever laid his heart so bare in an instrumental work. Robert and Clara particularly loved this Andante. The finale, however, was one of the very few movements where they thought Brahms betrayed his inexperience in handling larger forms: he quickly revised it, in deference to their judgement.

Excitement mounted towards the middle of October when Joachim arrived unexpectedly for a day. This gave Schumann an idea: why should not he, Brahms and Dietrich jointly compose a violin sonata to welcome Joachim back on the 27th when he was due as soloist at the first of the new season's subscription concerts? Response to the challenge was immediate. Dietrich and Brahms assumed responsibility for the first movement and Scherzo, respectively, while Schumann took over the Intermezzo and finale. For unity, they agreed on the notes F A E as an underlying motto theme. This came from Joachim's personal motto 'Frei aber einsam' (free but lonely), to which Brahms eventually grew to retort 'Frei aber froh' (free but happy), often working the notes F A F into his own compositions as if to prove that he meant it.

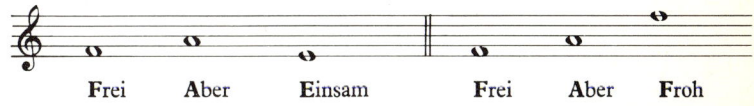

4 Joachim's F A E motto. Brahms's F A F motto.

3 Andante from Piano Sonata in C, Op. 1 (1852–3) showing how Brahms's melody often grew from folk-song.

First Travels

Joachim himself, with Clara as his partner, gave the first performance at a festive gathering in the Schumanns' house on 28 October. When requested to guess the authorship of each movement, Joachim was right each time.

Brahms's highly-charged Scherzo (the only movement regularly heard today) rekindled Schumann's enthusiasm enough for him to write to Leipzig's famous publishing house, Breitkopf und Härtel, recommending that they looked at anything Brahms had to offer. But it was not until rejoining Joachim in Hanover, early in November, that Brahms realized the full impact he had made on his warm and generous Düsseldorf host: it was then, about a week after its appearance, that he read the article 'Neue Bahnen', ('New Paths'), which after nearly ten years' retirement from music criticism, Schumann had written for the *Neue Zeitschrift für Musik*, the progressive music magazine he had founded as a young man. Referring first to a number of gifted youngsters who had impressed him, Schumann continued:

> I felt certain an individual would suddenly emerge fated to give expression to the times in the highest and most ideal manner, who would achieve mastery not step by step, but at once, springing like Minerva fully armed from the head of Jove. And now here he is, a young man at whose cradle graces and heroes stood watch. His name is Johannes Brahms. . . . Even in his external appearance he displays those characteristics which proclaim: here is a man of destiny! Seated at the piano he began to disclose most wondrous regions. It was also most wondrous playing, which made of the piano an orchestra of mourning or jubilant voices. There were sonatas, more like disguised symphonies; songs, whose poetry would be intelligible even to one who didn't know the words, although a profound vocal line flows through them all; a few piano pieces, partly of a demoniac character, charmingly formed; then sonatas for violin and piano, string quartets, etc. – all so different from one another that each seemed to flow from a separate source. And finally it seemed as though he himself, a surging stream incarnate, swept them all together into a single waterfall, sending aloft a peaceful rainbow above the turbulent waves, flanked on the shores by playful butterflies and the voices of nightingales. When once he lowers his magic wand over the massed resources of chorus and orchestra, we shall have in store for us wonderful insights into the secret of the spiritual world. May the highest genius lend him strength for this!

Brahms's first letter to Breitkopf & Härtel, 8 November 1853

    Awed as well as thrilled, Brahms self-critically revised the manuscripts he himself thought worthy of publication before going to Leipzig to play them to Dr. Härtel, and to taste the first fruits of notoriety in one of Germany's greatest musical centres. Previously a nobody, he arrived to find himself the person everyone wanted to meet and to hear, if only, as a butt for the anti-Schumannites in Leipzig's faction-ridden musical circles. Even Liszt and Berlioz turned up when he was invited to play his C major Sonata and E flat minor Scherzo at one of the Gewandhaus chamber concerts. But Christmas away from home was unthinkable. By 20 December he was back with his family, his teachers and his friends in Hamburg, basking in their obvious pride. Exuberantly, he even made a round of all the familiar old sailors' taverns which not so very long ago had been his main stand-by in guaranteeing a weekly contribution to the family purse.

III *Heart-ache*

By early January, Brahms was back in Hanover in lodgings of his own, a cheque from his recently acquired publishers helping him to pay his way, and his mind teeming with ideas for a new Piano Trio in B major. Besides Joachim, he now found Julius Otto Grimm, a young musician who had warmly befriended him in Leipzig, living there too. The three of them also greatly enjoyed a visit from Hans von Bülow, at that time a budding young concert pianist much interested in what Brahms was writing for the piano. Excitement reached its peak towards the end of the month when Robert and Clara Schumann arrived to hear performances of Schumann's *Paradise and the Peri*, his Fourth Symphony and the Phantasie for violin and orchestra recently written for Joachim. As well as playing the solo part in the Phantasie, Joachim also conducted the symphony and Beethoven's 'Emperor', with Clara as soloist in the concerto. Informally, they all often met for chamber music together, besides enjoying a lot of good eating, drinking (Clara's diary specifically mentions Joachim's champagne) and conversation, with Schumann in unusually lively, reminiscent mood.

> Through the visit of the Schumanns we have had some delightful days here. What shall I tell you about them? Since then everything here seems to have real life in it, and that means a good deal. As a rule, there is nothing living at Hanover. Give my warmest greetings to that noble and delightful pair

was how Brahms described it all soon afterwards in a letter to Dietrich at Düsseldorf.

Less than a month later, the blow fell. Picking up the *Cologne Gazette*, Joachim read of Schumann's mental breakdown and abortive attempt to drown himself in the Rhine. 'Dear Dietrich,' Joachim wrote, 'if you bear the least friendship for Brahms and me, relieve us from our misery, and write immediately whether Schumann's state is really as serious as the papers say.'

On 3 March, Brahms arrived in Düsseldorf to find out for himself. As Clara's diary put it, 'he said he had only come to comfort me with music if I had any wish for it. He is going to stay here for the present, and later, when Robert is so far recovered that he can see strangers, he will devote himself to him. What touching friendship!' By 4 March Schumann's condition had sufficiently deteriorated to necessitate removal to a private asylum at Endenich, near Bonn. Clara, now far advanced in pregnancy, and with six young children to care for already, was alone and desperate, which brought Joachim to Düsseldorf on 5 March, and Grimm three days later.

In the weeks that followed, the others came and went, as their professional engagements permitted. Brahms, being free, stayed on. No one, not even Joachim, had done more for him than Schumann: this was the chance to show his gratitude. So long as he could do anything to relieve the strain for Clara, such as making music for or with her, reading to her (particularly his beloved E. T. A. Hoffmann), taking over any of her lessons if she felt unwell, amusing the children, sorting out Schumann's books and scores, or carrying messages to and from Endenich, all thoughts of furthering his own career (and at one moment towards the end of 1853, Joachim and Gisela von Arnim had suspected he might have been too self-seeking) were forgotten.

> That good Brahms always shows himself a most sympathetic friend. He does not say much, but one can see in his face, in his speaking eye, how he grieves with me for the loved one he so highly reveres. Besides, he is so kind in seizing every opportunity of cheering me by any means of anything musical. From so young a man I cannot but be doubly conscious of the sacrifice, for a sacrifice it undoubtedly is for anyone to be with me now

Clara confessed in her diary on 10 April.

On 11 June Clara's child was born. Felix was the chosen name, after Mendelssohn, and Brahms agreed to be one of the god-parents though it was decided that the christening ceremony itself should wait in case Schumann himself might be well enough to attend. Relieved and rejuvenated after the birth, Clara resumed her musical activities with new energy, sharing her discoveries and reactions with Brahms as

Heart-ache

spontaneously as she used to with her husband. Shortly before setting off for a holiday in Ostend in August, friends even reproached her about being too careless about her 'dignity as an artist' in her free and easy camaraderie with him. Brahms laid bare his own feelings with unusual frankness in a letter written from Ulm to his old Winsen friend, Herr Blume, on 16 August:

> Frau Schumann went with a friend on the 10th of this month to Ostend for the benefit of her health. I, after much persuasion, resolved to make a journey through Swabia during her absence. I did not know how greatly I was attached to the Schumanns, how I lived in them; everything seemed barren and empty to me, every day I wished to turn back, and was obliged to travel by rail in order to get quickly to a distance and forget about turning back. It was of no use; I have come as far as Ulm, partly on foot, partly by rail; I am going to return quickly, and would rather wait for Frau Schumann in Düsseldorf than wander about in the dark. When one has found such divine people as Robert and Clara Schumann, one should stick to them and

A page from the manuscript of Brahm's Variations on a Theme by Schumann, Op. 9 (1854)

not leave them, but raise and inspire one's self by them. The dear Schumann continues to improve, as you have read in my letter to my parents. There has been a great deal of gossip about his condition. I consider the best description of him is to be found in some of the works of E. T. A. Hoffmann (Rath Krespel, Serapion, and especially the splendid Kreisler, etc.). He has only stripped off his body too soon.

To greet Clara on her return, knowing special comfort would be needed on her wedding anniversary, Brahms had written a set of keyboard variations on Schumann's F sharp minor *Bunte Blätter* ('Variegated Leaves'), a theme of great personal significance for both Robert and Clara (she herself had recently composed variations on it) while cunningly interweaving one or two other quotations from their music into his own variations. He had specially coached her two eldest daughters, Marie and Elise, so that they could play Schumann's *Bilder aus Osten* ('Pictures from the East') duets to her 'wonderfully well'. He also shared all her emotion when she wrote to, and received a rational reply from, her husband, their first contact permitted since the breakdown. Yet as October wore on and Clara prepared to resume her platform career, for her financial position was now becoming precarious, Brahms's ache at the impending separation at lást told him the shattering truth. Suddenly he realized that his desire to remain in Düsseldorf was no longer prompted by compassion: he loved Clara with an all-consuming devotion never experienced in his life before – Clara who was fourteen years his senior and the wife of his greatest champion.

When her tour took her to Hamburg in November, he was able to meet her there, introduce her to his parents and to Marxsen, and show her his beloved collection of tin soldiers, still carefully preserved in the family cupboard. Though not this time accepting Frau Brahms's invitation to stay (that came about when she returned the following spring), Clara ate several meals with the family, finding them 'simple folk, but worthy of all respect. . . . I always enjoy unaffected bourgeois life of this kind.' In her diary she nevertheless marvelled anew as to 'how it was possible for Johannes to develop into what he is, amidst such surroundings, when he had to do everything for himself'.

By this time Clara was regularly including pieces by Brahms in her recital programmes, particularly the Andante and Scherzo of the F minor Sonata. 'Why did you not allow me to learn to play the flute so that I could travel with you?' he wrote to her. 'Just think, I could have arranged the Andante from the F minor Sonata

Heart-ache

for flute, guitar and kettle-drum and I and Frl. Schönerstedt and Pfund could have serenaded you.' Christmas 1854 brought a reunion with Clara and all the children (it was Brahms's first Christmas away from home, worrying Clara enough for her to write an assuaging letter to his mother), by which time she had agreed to call him 'du' in her letters, in response to his own confused endearments – often disguised, as in the letter about the flute, in brave youthful humour. 'I could not refuse, for indeed I love him like a son,' so her diary put it.

Improvement in Schumann's health at the turn of the year made it possible for both Joachim and Brahms to visit him in person. For Clara, there were the most lucid letters Schumann had yet written, full of admiration for Brahms's Variations and a still newer set of four Ballades for piano, as well as expressions of personal affection quite as deep for Brahms as for Clara and his own children. Brahms's own loyalty to his old champion remained unshakeable. But when Clara had to leave for a Dutch tour in mid-January, he travelled with her and her companion as far as Emmerich to say goodbye, only to turn up in Rotterdam two days later. 'He quite frightened me at first,' Clara's diary reveals, 'But afterwards I gave myself up to the truest joy.'

There were other red letter days in 1855, too, such as in early April when they went to Cologne together to hear Beethoven's *Missa Solemnis*; also Brahms's twenty-second birthday at Düsseldorf in May: 'he was very merry and thoroughly enjoyed it,' Clara wrote, "so that I too seemed to grow younger, for he whirled me along with him and I have not spent so cheerful a day since Robert fell ill.' Best of all was the week in July when, accompanied by one of Clara's female friends, they set out in hot sunshine for a walking tour by the Rhine, with Brahms gallantly carrying all immediate essentials for the journey in a rucksack on his back. On returning to Düsseldorf he helped Clara to move into a new apartment, where he was offered a 'charmingly cosy room' in which he could always stay – previously he had relied on nearby lodgings.

But it was a time of anguish too. After illusory improvement, Schumann's condition was now slowly beginning to deteriorate. Too proud to consider offers of financial help, Clara had to accept more and more concert engagements that took her away for weeks on end. For Brahms, even their precious moments of reunion were never wholly carefree: it was impossible to forget that lonely sufferer at Endenich. Money problems were growing acute, too. Pupils were not easy to find in Düsseldorf. His secret hopes that he might be asked to take over the

Brahms at the piano, 1856

Heart-ache

directorship of the town's music, now that the prospect of Schumann's recovery was fading, were finally dashed when the job went to the former deputy, Julius Tausch. Meanwhile Marxsen, sometimes even Brahms's parents too, were at a loss to understand his apparent inactivity over composition. After such an early flourish of trumpets from Schumann, they felt he ought to be doing a lot more to prove himself.

In the autumn Clara intervened by encouraging him to work hard again at the piano. She even decided to launch him in Danzig by inviting him to share in one or two of her recitals with Joachim. From there he went on alone to Bremen, Hamburg and Leipzig to play concertos by Beethoven (Nos. 4 and 5) and Mozart, also solos including Bach's Chromatic Fantasy and Fugue and Schumann's C major Fantasie, Op. 17, with reasonable, even if not outstanding, acclaim. But a letter to Clara from Hamburg in November shows that he was already obsessed with thoughts of the promised Düsseldorf Christmas reunion:

> While I am here, I often pass a shop in which I have discovered the most beautiful soldiers. Yesterday I went in to buy an acrobat for Felix, and at the same time to have a look at them. . . . At present I have the most fascinating battle-piece I ever saw, with a little tower

as well. I am overjoyed with it. At Christmas I will set out all my troops so beautifully that you will be delighted with them.

With Clara up and away again even before the end of the year, Brahms wandered restlessly between Düsseldorf, Leipzig, Hamburg or wherever the odd concert engagement took him. In the spring he met the distinguished uprising baritone, Julius Stockhausen, and gave one or two recitals with him. Meanwhile news from Endenich grew graver each month. Only a week after Clara left for England (their 'hardest parting of all') Brahms had to write to tell her, as gently as possible, that the doctors had given up all hope. By May he was grieving so much that on his twenty-third birthday his mother wrote 'Johannes dear, if we only had the power to do something for the good Schumann! I beg you not to take it too much to heart; you cannot help him, and it only does you harm.' But it was Brahms alone, of a group of visitors, who was allowed to see Schumann on his forty-sixth birthday in June. And when a telegram came to say the end was near, it was he who escorted Clara to Endenich for the last farewell – she had never been allowed to visit her husband before – and who sustained her through the last few anguished days before Schumann's death on 29 July. At the funeral in Bonn on 31 July, Brahms, carrying a laurel wreath, walked with Joachim and Dietrich in front of the coffin. 'With his departure, all my happiness is over. A new life is beginning for me' wrote Clara that night in her diary.

Escape was now essential for them all. So accompanied by Clara's two eldest surviving sons of seven and eight, and Brahms's twenty-five-year-old sister, Elise, they set off for a month's holiday in Switzerland only a fortnight later.

For Clara and Brahms it was the great moment of truth. For two and a half years he had worshipped her. Though constantly struggling to pretend to herself that her feelings were only maternal, she loved him too. But she had worshipped Robert since she was a child, and on his death-bed he had recognized her and put his arm round her. Nor could Brahms forget all that Schumann had done for him. Wandering together in the mountains by the Lake of Lucerne, they realized that nothing was changed by death, that they could never belong to each other as man and wife. By 13 September they were back in Düsseldorf, older, wiser and sadder. With her fourteen years' extra experience, Clara knew better than Brahms that for the time being it would be better to go their own separate ways. But her diary entry for 21 October reveals what the renunciation cost her: 'Johannes left, I went to the station with him – as I came back I felt as if I were returning from a funeral.'

In so far as the outside world knew, Brahms had only written one or two sets of variations, four Ballades (Op. 10), and a few smaller gigues, sarabandes and fugues (the last primarily as exercises) for piano while at Clara's side. But throughout these storm-tossed months he had secretly been in the grips of impulses far more powerful than anything he had ever previously experienced, so powerful that he scarcely even knew how to begin trying to grapple with them on manuscript paper. It all started when only a month after learning of Schumann's attempted suicide in the Rhine, he went to Cologne to hear Beethoven's Choral Symphony for the first time in his life. Under the double impact, all he could do was to get down something of what he felt in the form of a sonata for two pianos, significantly borrowing Beethoven's key of D minor. Though it was more or less complete by the end of May, 1854, he still felt that two pianos alone were not really capable of conveying ideas so powerful, and almost at once he began to recast the work as a symphony. Not till 1856 did he eventually realize that only by throwing orchestra and piano into conflict could he really express the mighty forces of fate against which man pits his own little strength in vain. But even though sketched in this form before Brahms left Düsseldorf in the autumn of 1856, it was not till early 1859, after many revisions, that he allowed the world to hear it as his piano concerto No. 1 in D minor. In the

5 **Adagio from Piano Concerto in D minor, Op. 15,** occupying Brahms between 1854 and 1858. He subsequently told a friend this movement was a portrait of Clara.

Heart-ache

printed score there was not a word as to what initially inspired it: more than any of his romantic contemporaries, Brahms hated revealing his emotional secrets. But when in 1875, some twenty years later, he eventually revised and completed a Piano Quartet in C minor (Op. 60) which was also sketched (in C sharp minor) during these same chaotic youthful years, he did, just once, confess the truth to his publisher, Simrock: 'You might put a portrait on the title-page! A head with a pistol in front of it. Now you'll have some idea of the music. I will send you my photograph for that purpose! Can you also have a blue dress-coat, yellow pantaloons and top boots, as you seem to like colour-printing?' The reference was to the hero of Goethe's novel, *The Sorrows of Young Werther*, who shot himself because in love with the wife of his best friend. Though never again in life did Brahms ever betray quite so much in words, everything suggests that his First Symphony in C minor, not completed until 1876, grew from the same youthful trauma. As a man, the experience was to deprive him of domestic happiness for ever. As an artist, it was his baptism by fire, in time to make him one of the immortals.

Brahms's mother, Christiane, in later life

Brahms's father, Jakob, 1838

Brahms's sister, Elise, 1860

Brahms's brother, Fritz, 1870

Picking up the Threads IV

Though at Christmas, 1856, Brahms was back in Düsseldorf with Clara and the seven children he knew so well and often wrote little songs for, his parents' flat in Hamburg became the base from which he attempted to pick up the threads of an interrupted career – teaching, playing at the occasional concert, and composing avidly if circumstances permitted. When an invitation arrived to spend Whitsun 1857 with the von Meysenbug family in Detmold, so that the reigning Prince could look him over with a view to a possible court appointment, he jumped at the chance: the plan was hatched by Fräulein von Meysenbug, sister of Detmold's Hofmarschall, to whom Brahms had briefly given piano lessons at a time when Clara could not. The visit had its moments of social embarrassment, not least when Brahms and Fräulein von Meysenbug's young nephew, Carl, were observed sneaking back home at daybreak in bedraggled evening clothes from an all-night party after Brahms's court audition, culminating in a hill climb to watch the sun-rise. But his playing and general artistic integrity impressed the Prince, who, while recognizing that the young Hamburger was never likely to make an elegant courtier, offered him a three-month contract to start that October at the generous salary of 566 thalers (about £900 today), with free board and lodging at a pleasant nearby inn.

Official duties were not too onerous. He had to give piano lessons to the Princess Friederike, whom he always found sympathetic, and one or two of her friends. He was also expected to play regularly at the court concerts directed by the old Kapellmeister Kiel, with whom 'I hit it off somewhat better than not at all', he confided to Joachim. His concerto repertory by now included Mozart, Beethoven, Mendelssohn, Schumann, Chopin and Moscheles. Sometimes, too, he would play solos, or else chamber music with various members of the orchestra. He particularly liked the leader, Bargheer, who had once studied with Joachim, and often teased him when they rehearsed together by deliberately starting off in the wrong key – Brahms never lost his skill in transposing.

Last but not least, he had to conduct the regular practices of the Court choral society, in which the Prince and all his family sang, alongside music-lovers specially invited from outside the castle. This experience he found invaluable, for as he wrote to Joachim: 'What a small amount of practical knowledge I have! My stuff is written far too unpractically.' Old, sacred music found a place in the rehearsals, so did newer composers like Schumann. But naturally he gave them quite a few pieces of his own, too, including the *Marienlieder* ('Songs of the Virgin Mary'), described by him as 'in the manner of old German hymns and folk-songs', besides several more actual folk-song arrangements such as had gone down so well when as a boy, he had conducted the Men's Choir at Winsen. Though he rarely worried about distinguishing between genuine age-old *Volkslieder* ('Folk-songs') and more recently composed tunes imitating the folk-song style, his love for all this great fund of simple German melody and verse grew even stronger now that he felt so close to its roots when wandering off on long afternoon walks in the beautiful Teutoburger forest nearby.

During the mornings, he allowed nothing to disturb his composition. Besides choral music, his mind also began to turn to instrumental serenades. He was always acutely sensitive to atmosphere, and somehow the rigid formalities of castle life made him feel that he was back again in the age of Haydn and Mozart, when providing simple, extrovert entertainment music for 'their Excellencies' was a prime requisite. But as a North German, and also an intensely self-critical student of Marxsen, Brahms could not approach even this comparatively uninvolved task lightly. His first Serenade in D did not emerge as he really wanted it until 1860, after three years' metamorphosis from a shortish nonet for wind and strings into a six-movement work for full orchestra. Its successor in A (his favourite, with unusually dark sonority because of his omission of violins) appeared in 1859, but it, too, was substantially revised some fifteen years later. After storm-tossed Düsseldorf, Detmold in fact began to seem like some strange, other-worldly retreat, outside time and reality. He appreciated its security, and still more the peace of its forests, enough to return for similar three-month periods at the end of 1858 and 1859. But apart from the Princess Friederike, Bargheer and

Brahms's lodgings at Hamm

Picking up the Threads

Carl von Meysenbug, he felt too bereft of kindred spirits to consider settling there, as the Prince no doubt hoped he might as soon as old Kapellmeister Kiel retired. 'It's really just as if I had emigrated,' he told Joachim. Despite Hamburg's noisy streets, he was always glad when he could get back to its lively artistic activity and to his own circle of friends in the wider musical world.

Thanks to Jakob's improved professional status and the money Brahms himself could contribute, they now lived in a larger flat at Fuhlentwiethe 74, where Brahms had a bed-sitter able to accommodate such essentials as a piano, a writing-desk, his cherished collection of tin soldiers, and the very considerable library he had accumulated over the years, including quite a few old rarities picked up in antiquarian bookshops. But he still felt the atmosphere too suffocating for work, and began to think longingly of all the lovely houses in rural surroundings only just about a half hour's walk from the city gates. Eventually he found just what he wanted in the suburb of Hamm, where a certain Frau Dr. Rösing, aunt of two singers he knew, rented him a large room with a balcony overlooking the garden. 'It is beautiful out here at Hamm: the sun shines so brightly in my rooms that, if I did not see the bare trees through the window, I should believe it was summer,' he wrote to his friend Dietrich, and soon afterwards, 'Everything is in blossom now, and out here at Hamm it is simply a treat to listen to the nightingales singing amongst the budding trees.'

Picking up the Threads

In these congenial new surroundings amidst music-loving friends and neighbours, and with contacts renewed with the town's professional musicians, he gradually began to feel 'a regular son of Hamburg' as he put it to Joachim. 'I'm content to let things take their course from day to day (only not so far as concerns your arrival). I am also busy teaching. One girl always plays better than the others, and some even play still worse.'

As regards live music-making, his main source of satisfaction came from a ladies' choir which he himself got together after hearing some of them sing an anthem at the wedding of a friend at which he played the organ. He gave his services without fee, and the practices were friendly and informal. But *Fix oder nix* (Up to the mark or nothing) was adopted as their motto, and insisting on regular attendance and punctuality he drew up a detailed set of rules in mock-official jargon of by-gone years, signed under his old pseudonym, Johannes Kreisler (junior). As a fine of eight shillings ('Hamburg currency') was imposed on offenders, his fourth clause explained, 'the money so collected shall be given to the poor, and it is desired that none of them get too much'. The fifth clause stipulated that 'manuscript music is largely confided to the discretion of the ladies. Wherefore it shall be preserved in due love and all kindness by the honourable and virtuous ladies, married or unmarried, as being the property of others, and shall also in no wise be taken outside the society'. This was really important, for Brahms's imagination at this

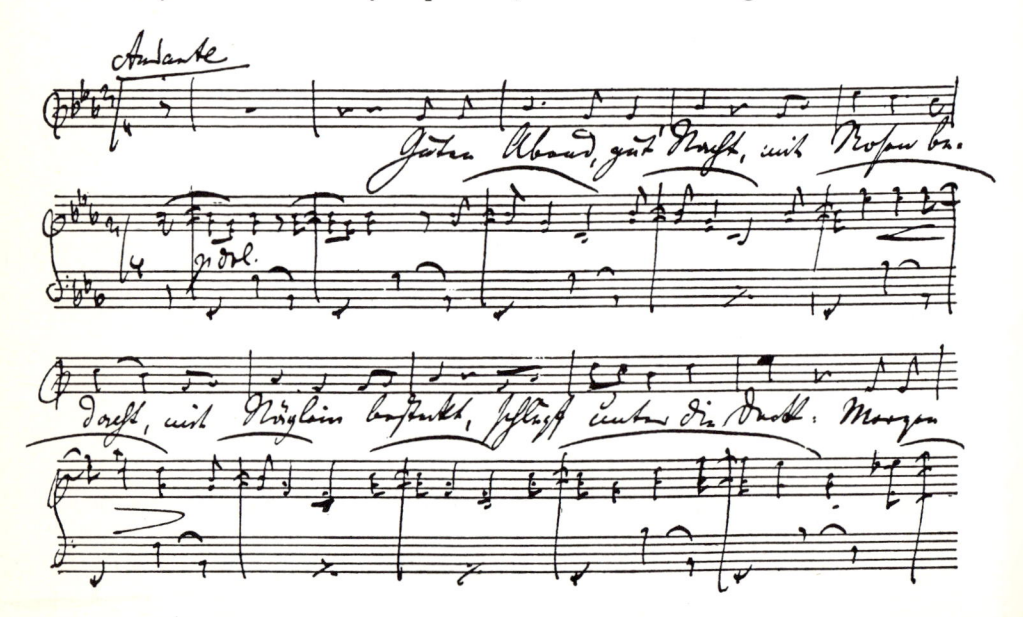

A page from the manuscript of 'Wiegenlied'

6 'Wiegenlied', Op. 49, No. 4.
Written for the birth of the first child of Frau Faber, who as Bertha Porubszky, was one of Brahms's favourite members of his Hamburg Ladies' Choir.

Zart bewegt

Gu-ten A-bend, gut' Nacht, mit Ro-sen be-dacht, mit Näg-lein be-steckt schlupf' un-ter die Deck': Mor-gen früh, wenn Gott will, wirst du wie-der ge-weckt, Mor-gen früh, wenn Gott will, wirst du wie-der ge-weckt.

In your cra-dle sleep sound, Red ro-ses a-round and pinks I will spread, to co-ver your bed: In the mor-ning the sun will in glo-ry a-rise, in the mor-ning a-gain God will o-pen your eyes.

time was inflamed by the sound of their fresh young voices and attractive company, resulting in a spate of new compositions for female choir, including the Op. 17. Partsongs with accompaniment for two horns and harp, as well as solo quartets and duets. Some of the quartets were rehearsed in the garden at Hamm, for Frau Rösing's nieces, Betty and Marie Völckers, were both in the choir's solo quartet, and lived with their father next door. When Clara Schumann came over to Hamburg for Brahms's birthday in May 1860, she joined the choir and its conductor 'for a delightful expedition in the steamer to Blankenese. When we got there we sought out the most beautiful trees in the garden and sang under them, Johannes sitting on a branch to conduct,' so her diary records.

Since the autumn of 1857 Clara had made her headquarters in Berlin to be near her mother; she worried less about the children, when away on tour, with a grandmother nearby. Though she and Brahms had dismissed all thoughts of a permanent union, the bond between them remained strong. Every new work Brahms wrote was immediately sent to Clara for criticism, and rarely a birthday, Christmas, Easter or summer holiday passed without an attempt to meet, preferably in company with close friends like Joachim, Grimm, Dietrich and others. During the hot summer of 1857 they were by the Rhine at Oberwesel and St. Goarshausen. The following year brought an even larger reunion in Göttingen, where Grimm had settled as music director, and married his young wife, Philippine. Mornings were usually given to work. But in the afternoons they would all meet for expeditions into the country, while in the evenings they liked nothing better than to make music together, particularly when there was something new from Brahms to try out. If a singer was needed, the Grimms often invited their friend, Agathe von Siebold, daughter of a professor at Göttingen University. She had a soprano voice which Joachim likened to the tone of an Amati violin, and Brahms loved to accompany her. Towards the end of September Grimm wrote to tell a friend that Brahms had composed 'ten glorious songs which Gathe sings to us, and we are all agreed this is a wonderful time'.

For Brahms, still only twenty-five, it was a disturbing new experience to be in close contact with an intelligent but also lively, carefree and physically attractive young girl of his own age; besides loving music, she shared his enthusiasm for long walks in the hills, and quite plainly adored him. After an ardent correspondence throughout his three

Picking up the Threads

months at Detmold he rushed back to see her early in the New Year with most of the songs of his Op. 14 and Op. 19 cycles now complete, while the Grimms and other Göttingen friends eagerly awaited the announcement of an engagement. When he left after a fortnight without having officially proposed, Grimm even rebuked him for not making his intentions plain. But inwardly Brahms was distressed: he could not banish memories of the previous summer when Clara, noticing the growing attraction between him and Agathe, suddenly sent her children back to Berlin and excused herself on the grounds of wanting to visit a friend in Düsseldorf. Conscience-stricken as he was about Agathe, now as hurt as she was baffled by his behaviour (when her father died a few years later, she even went off to Ireland as a governess to try and forget), he gradually realized that his loyalty to Clara was stronger than any passing longing for domesticity – a longing that incidentally always sharpened when close personal friends like Grimm and Dietrich got married. Three years later he met another charming young girl in Dietrich's house at Oldenburg, prompting the confession to his host: 'I like her, I should like to marry her; such a girl could also make me happy.' But again he held back. Clara sometimes upset him with her unrelenting efforts to canvas support for his works in the outside world. 'You demand too rapid and enthusiastic a recognition of talent which you happen to like,' he once remonstrated. He was also sometimes impatient with her lack of humour, her inability to understand that he often said outrageous things with a straight face just to pull her leg. She in her turn was often hurt by his moodiness and brusqueness. Yet scarcely a day passed for either of them without thought of the other. In the summer of 1861 he confessed that while he wrote the Allegretto of his G minor Piano Quartet he was thinking of her in every bar.

To Agathe he had pleaded, 'I love you, but I can't wear fetters.' Around 1864 he even set a poem by Platen (Op. 32, No. 5) with 'Shackle me not with your fetters' as its first line. Nevertheless to the world at large his explanation of his bachelorhood was usually that he could not bear the thought of having to involve a wife in his professional failures, and accept her pity. Excuse though it was, it at least made sense on the surface, for at the height of his entanglement with Agathe he had experienced the bitterest humiliation of his life when his D minor Piano Concerto, over which he had brooded for five years and which meant more to him than anything he had yet essayed, was pronounced a failure. The public were at least polite in Hanover, where he himself

Agathe von Siebold

gave the première on 22 January 1859, with Joachim conducting. But at the Leipzig Gewandhaus, where he played it under Rietz on 27 January, it was hissed. To his friends he put a brave face on the situation, claiming that his 'slight disappointment' quickly passed when the orchestra went on to play a Haydn symphony in C and Beethoven's *Ruins of Athens*. 'I think it is the best thing that can happen to anyone, it compels one to collect one's ideas thoroughly and brace one's courage. I am still experimenting and groping my way,' he wrote to Joachim, immediately betraying his underlying ache by adding, 'but the hissing was surely too much?' It was not until a performance conducted by Levi in Mannheim in 1865 that the German public at large showed true appreciation of the mighty drama of the first movement, directly inspired by Schumann's attempted suicide in the Rhine, the grave luminosity of the Adagio, over which, in Joachim's score, Brahms wrote 'Benedictus qui venit in nomine Domini' ('Blessed is he who comes in the name of the Lord') as indication that it was a portrait of Clara (Schumann's pupils often called him 'Domini'), or the exuberance of the finale, recalling Brahms's love for the popular music of Hungary first introduced to him by Reményi. Even his rejection of his original slow Scherzo, envisaged as a kind of sarabande, was eventually seen to be a stroke of genius: redrafted, it was to find a much more fitting place in his *German Requiem*. But to Leipzig concert-goers of 1859, a concerto involving mind as well as fingers was unthinkable. For them, Brahms's work was infinitely too symphonic. Forgetting every lesson taught by Mozart and Beethoven, they jibbed at the idea of the solo instrument being woven into the musical argument instead of used merely for virtuoso display.

The press was almost as damning as the general public. But the *Neue Zeitschrift für Musik* stood apart, conceding that, 'notwithstanding its considerable want of outward effect, we regard the poetic content of the concerto as an unmistakable sign of significant and original creative powers'. Encouragement from this quarter was surprising, for though Schumann had originally founded the paper to rout the Philistines and hasten a new poetic age, its current editor, Franz Brendel, had gone to extremes Schumann never dreamed of, making it the mouthpiece of the New German school led by Liszt and Wagner. The way these and other *avant-garde* composers were using music to tell stories or paint pictures was anathema to Brahms, who always dissolved all his own emotion into pure music. Like Goethe he believed that, in so far as the outside world was concerned, music should begin where words end. When the *Neue Zeitschrift* celebrated its twenty-fifth anniversary in 1859 without any invitation to Clara, the founder's wife, and then published an article claiming that every musician of note in Germany upheld the principles of the New German school, Brahms could no longer contain himself – despite this paper's comparative kindness to his Concerto. With Joachim's help he drew up a manifesto of protest early in 1860 which he hoped to get signed by enough influential musicians to put the *Neue Zeitschrift* to shame.

Picking up the Threads

> The undersigned have long followed with regret the pursuits of a certain party, whose organ is Brendel's *Zeitschrift für Musik*. The above journal continually spreads the view that musicians of more serious endeavour are fundamentally in accord with the tendencies it represents, that they recognize in the compositions by the leaders of this group works of artistic value and that altogether, and especially in north Germany, the contentions for and against the so-called music of the future are concluded, and the dispute settled in its favour. To protest against such a misrepresentation of facts is regarded as their duty by the undersigned, and they declare that, so far at least as they are concerned, the principles stated by Brendel's journal are not recognized, and that they regard the productions of the leaders and pupils of the so-called 'New German' school, which in part simply reinforce these principles in practice and in part again enforce new and unheard-of theories, as contrary to the innermost spirit of music, strongly to be deplored and condemned.
>
>   Johannes Brahms   Joseph Joachim
>   Julius Otto Grimm   Bernhard Scholz.

Unfortunately for Brahms, the document somehow found its way into print in the Berlin *Echo* when only these four signatures had been added. Apart from Grimm, who was thirty-three, the rest of them were still in their twenties, with little to show for themselves in comparison with older luminaries like Liszt and Wagner. All it did for Brahms was to earn him mild derision at a moment when his self-confidence had been undermined enough already, and drive him to adopt a far more extreme anti-romantic pose than he genuinely felt.

His luck was out in another way too. Secretly he had hoped that when Friedrich Grund retired, the city fathers might offer him the conductorship of the Hamburg Philharmonic Society and of the Singakademie. But the job went to his singer friend, Stockhausen. 'This is a much sadder business for me than you think, or can perhaps understand. As I am altogether rather an old-fashioned person, so I am in this, that I am not a cosmopolitan, but love my native town as a mother,' he wrote to Clara, a few months after a happy, productive summer fortnight with her and Dietrich at the foot of the Ebernburg, near Münster am Stein. 'You are still so young, dear Johannes, you will find an abiding place yet,' she replied to him in Vienna, not realizing that the city he was then visiting for the first time in his life would prove just that.

The Lure of Vienna   V

Brahms himself certainly had no idea that he would one day live in Vienna: that idea did not begin to take definite shape for another six or seven years. During this first visit, lasting till the spring of 1863, he was often homesick for the city which had just rejected his services. But he quickly felt the attraction of the Austrian capital. As he wrote to a friend in March 1863:

> I have spent a whole winter here, very much at a loose end, but rather enjoyably and cheerfully. I regret above all things that I didn't know Vienna before. The gaiety of the town, the beauty of the surroundings, the sympathetic and vivacious public, how stimulating all these are to the artist! In addition we have in particular the sacred memory of the great musicians whose lives and work are brought daily to our minds. In the case of Schubert especially one has the impression of his being still alive. Again and again one meets people who talk of him as of a good friend: again and again one comes across new works, the existence of which was unknown and which are so untouched that one can scrape the very writing-sand off them.

Geiringer recounts that Brahms did this very often, carefully preserving the sand in a little box. Schubert's Easter Cantata, *Lazarus*, was one of his most thrilling personal discoveries.

On first arriving Brahms was welcomed by several old friends from Hamburg singing circles who now lived in Vienna. But he quickly made contact with a more cosmopolitan group of musicians, including the composer, Peter Cornelius, the musicologist, Nottebohm, and the brilliant young pianist, Karl Tausig, enjoying their relish of food and drink as much as their intellectual stimulation. Through Tausig he briefly met Wagner, and though never an uncritical admirer, generously helped to copy out orchestral parts of extracts from *Meistersinger* then scheduled, amongst selections from other Wagner operas, for concert performance in Vienna. 'Unassuming and good-natured, but he showed little vivacity and was often hardly noticed at our gatherings,' was Wagner's subsequent description of this encounter. As a composer, Wagner always thought Brahms too tradition-bound, too reluctant to surprise or startle. Yet after hearing Brahms play his recently completed *Handel Variations*, even Wagner had to concede: 'That shows what may still be done with the old forms provided someone appears who knows how to treat them.'

These piano variations and the two Piano Quartets in G minor and A major (1861–2) were the works in which Brahms chose to present himself (assisted by members of Vienna's well-known Hellmesberger Quartet) to the Viennese public at large during that first winter. Some of his songs and part-songs were included in other programmes, and he had the still greater satisfaction of hearing both his orchestral Serenades played at concerts of the Gesellschaft der Musikfreunde and the Philharmonic Society. As always there were some dissenting voices. Yet his general success was such that no sooner had he returned to Hamburg in May, after a flying visit to Hanover to hear Joachim's new singer wife, Amalie Weiss, in Gluck's *Orfeo* (Brahms was always strongly drawn tothe contralto voice), than an invitation arrived from Vienna to return in the early autumn as conductor of its Singakademie.

Having always enjoyed working with choirs, Brahms could not resist this new challenge from a group specializing in old church music and unaccompanied singing, the more so since only the previous year they had made history by giving Bach's *St. Matthew Passion* in Vienna for the first time. Bach also figured prominently in Brahms's programmes during the winter of 1863/4, including the first performance in Vienna of the *Christmas Oratorio*. Schumann's *Requiem für Mignon* was another work he introduced to the city, besides finding a place for older rarities by composers including Schütz, Gabrieli, and even the Englishmen, Bennet and Morley. The choir sometimes complained of the difficulty of all the new music they had to learn, and the press of the extent to which they betrayed this fact at concerts, but a programme of Brahms's own music towards the end of the season pleased most people, especially his folk-song arrangements. Yet although the initial contract was for three years, Brahms resigned at the end of the first season. As he explained to a friend, 'While in any other city a regular position is desirable, in Vienna one lives better without it. The many interesting people, the libraries, the Burgtheater, the picture galleries, all these give me enough to do and enjoy outside one's own room.'

Besides wanting more time for his own composing and playing, as well as freedom to visit friends whenever the old *Wanderlust* overtook him, Brahms at this moment was also deeply concerned about his parents, and anxious to return home to try and sort out their problems. His father, recently admitted to the Hamburg Philharmonic Orchestra, had gradually grown tired of a woman seventeen years his senior, the more so since she could not endure the extra practice he now had to do at home. Though a reasonably successful piano teacher, Fritz would accept no financial responsibility. So it fell to Brahms, albeit far from well-off, to install his mother and Elise in a small apartment of their own while his father took a room elsewhere. Loving both parents dearly, Brahms always hoped for a reconciliation. As he wrote to his father in October 1864:

> That mother and Elise have reserved a room for me would please me indeed if I could think that you would occupy it frequently! I hope that this will be the case. You can often take your afternoon nap in the company of my books. Don't stint Mother as regards my money; it is not important that it should last until the New Year, and money can bring a smile to many a face which would otherwise frown. Do your best, even if things should be unpleasant at times.

But a return to the old family life, with the traditional egg-nog to which Brahms often referred in letters home, was not to be. In early February 1865 he received a telegram from Fritz to say that, shortly after a stroke, their mother had died.

Brahms was heart-broken. Though now almost thirty-two, he had never outgrown the need of her solicitude and love. But his grief sharpened an urge that had been with him ever since the death of Robert Schumann. This was to compose a Requiem using not the traditional Latin text, overawed by the terror of the Day of Judgement, but with words from the German Bible specially selected by himself to console the living. The kind of divine comfort he wished to convey was specific enough for him to reject a friend's advice as to how the text could be given a more conventionally religious slant. 'I dispensed with passages such as St. John's Gospel, Ch. 3, verse 16,* with all knowledge and

---

*'For God so loved the world, that he gave his only begotten Son, that whosoever believeth in him should not perish, but have everlasting life.'

The Lure of Vienna

intention,' was his reply. A Bible-lover and believer in Christian ethics, he was never able to accept the Church's insistence on personal redemption through the Crucifixion.

Getting the work into musical shape was as long and heart-searching

7 German Requiem, second movement, originally conceived as a slow Scherzo for the D minor Piano Concerto.

Langsam, marschmässig

Denn al - - les Fleisch es ist wie Gras und al - - le
Be - hold all flesh is as the grass, and all the

Herr - lich - keit des Men - - schen wie des Gra - ses
good - li - ness of man is as the flower of

a task as all his major projects always were. For the second movement of the Requiem Brahms in fact turned to the Sarabande he had originally intended as a slow scherzo for his D minor Piano Concerto, conceived in embryo immediately after Schumann's attempted suicide. To the words, 'Behold, all flesh is as the grass', it is like a nobly resigned funeral march before the *Requiem*'s third movement which, after a sombre, introspective start for the baritone soloist, culminates in a great fugue, anchored to a low D throughout, to the words, 'But the righteous souls are in the hands of God'. Again in the penultimate movement Brahms uses fugue as a symbol of divine order, as Beethoven in later life so often did before him.

When the first three movements were tried out in Vienna at the end of 1867, their effect was undermined by the drummer who played the sustained low D in the third movement's fugal ending *fortissimo* throughout. But this time Brahms was undeterred. He believed in what he had to say, and confidently awaited the official première of the *German Requiem*, as it was to be called, which he had promised to conduct in Bremen Cathedral, with Stockhausen as baritone soloist, on Good Friday, 10 April 1868.

The choir (including his much loved ladies' quartet from Hamburg) had been excellently rehearsed by Dr. Reinthaler, the cathedral organist and choirmaster. All those nearest and dearest to Brahms were there to uphold him, including his father and Clara, whom he proudly escorted by arm up the nave to her seat. Somehow everyone realized that with his thirty-fifth birthday barely a month away, this was the moment when his true stature would at last declare itself to the world. Clara's diary captures the atmosphere best:

> As I saw Johannes standing there, baton in hand, I could not help thinking of my dear Robert's prophecy, 'Let him but once grasp the magic wand and work with orchestra and choirs', which is fulfilled today. The baton was really a magic wand and its spell was upon all present, even upon his bitterest enemies. It was a joy such as I have not felt for a long time. After the performance there was a supper in the Rathskeller, at which everyone was jubilant – it was like a musical festival. Reinthaler made a speech about Johannes which so moved me that (unfortunately!!!) I burst into tears. I thought of Robert, and what joy it would have been to him if he could have lived to see it. . . .

Elated as Brahms himself was, he was still not completely satisfied. Perhaps because the first and second halves of the work had been separated by miscellaneous items in the cathedral, including solos from *Messiah* and the *St. Matthew Passion* sung by Amalie Joachim, he soon added an extra movement (No. 5) to the six already heard, in the form of an idyllic soprano solo, like consolation from heaven, to the words, 'And ye now are sorrowful. As one whom his mother comforteth, so will I

Brahms in 1870

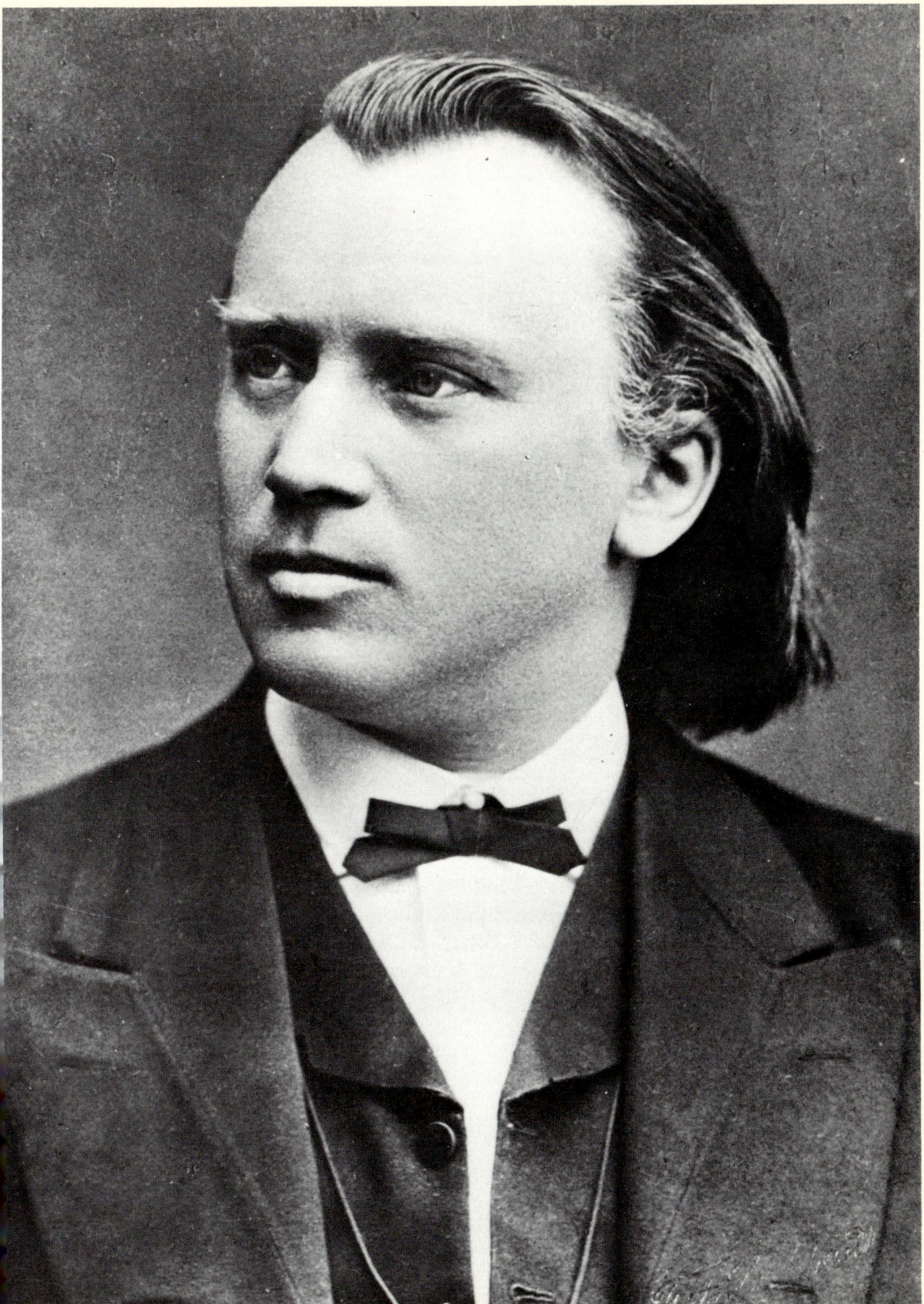

comfort you.' In this definitive, seven-movement version, the *German Requiem* had its première in Leipzig in February 1869.

By this time the circle of friends with whom Brahms could always go and stay was growing rapidly, not least in Switzerland, which had already taken as strong a hold on him, for its natural beauty, as his music had on it. Here, he met Mathilde Wesendonck (immortalized by Wagner in *Tristan und Isolde*) who offered him a cottage to work in whenever he wanted it, also the great surgeon and music-lover, Theodor Billroth, later to become one of his intimates in Vienna, and eventually, the poet, Joseph Widmann, who perhaps appreciated the true nature of Brahms's often underestimated intellect (he rarely expressed his deepest thoughts and feelings in casual company) better than most people.

But Brahms's favourite retreat was now Lichtental, near Baden-Baden, where in 1863 Clara Schumann had bought a charming house which she kept as a holiday home until 1879. Renting modest rooms of his own, looking out on to wooded mountain slopes, he loved to get up at four or five o'clock and roam in the hills to watch the sunrise before settling down to a morning's work. His lunch was usually taken at some local inn: at the 'Bär', where he was very well known, he sometimes dropped in early for a gossip while helping them to prepare the vegetables. He was invariably at Clara's house for four o'clock coffee, often served on her balcony, and there was always a place laid for him, on her right, for the evening meal. If Clara had to go away, he sometimes took over any specially talented pupil. When his subsequent English biographer, Florence May, once found herself entrusted to him, she particularly valued his advice about muscular relaxation, and his rejection of mechanical studies by Czerny and others in favour of exercises made out of actual pieces they were working at, with difficult passages accented in different rhythms to strengthen weak fingers. No lesson was deemed complete without substantial recourse to Bach: he also never allowed her to forget that miracles could be achieved by wandering in the forests, or reading Goethe. If his own works were ever studied, he always insisted on a full, deep bass. But he had no use for the metronome. As he subsequently wrote to his friend, Henschel (in the context of the *Requiem*),

> I think here as well as with all other music the metronome is of no value. As far at least as my experience goes, everybody has, sooner or

Theodor Billroth

later, withdrawn his metronome marks. Those which can be found in my works, good friends have talked me into putting there. I myself have never believed that my blood and a mechanical instrument go well together.

For his own musical pleasure, Brahms was never happier than when Johann Strauss, Vienna's waltz-king, gave seasons with his orchestra on the terrace of Baden's Kurhaus: serious-minded North German as he was, he adored popular Viennese music just as much as that of the Hungarian gypsies: he frequently confessed that he would have given anything in the world to have written the *Blue Danube*. Proximity to Baden and Karlsruhe, both notable resorts, also ensured a constant stream of eminent visitors to Clara's house, including the singer, Pauline Viardot and her friend, the Russian writer, Turgenev, also the

8 Waltz in E major from Op. 39, originally written for piano duet, but later arranged by Brahms as a piano solo.

The Lure of Vienna

Russian pianist, Anton Rubinstein. As a lot of good instrumentalists lived and worked nearby, many of Brahms's new works were tried out and discussed at these happy, informal gatherings. For piano there were the *Hexenvariationen*, as Clara nicknamed what the world now knows as the devilishly difficult *Paganini Variations*, and the *Hungarian Dances* for piano duet, which invariably aroused delirious enthusiasm whenever Brahms and Clara played them together. In the chamber music sphere there were the Piano Quintet in F minor (characteristically going through preliminary phases of existence as a string quintet and a sonata for two pianos before Brahms found the perfect medium), the Second String Sextet in G, into which he remorsefully wove a theme made out of the musical letters of the name Agathe, a Cello Sonata (No. 1) in E minor, and last but not least a Horn Trio (Op. 40) the opening idea of which came to him while wandering in the forests above Baden – several years later he showed his friend, Dietrich, the exact spot.

Whether due to discussions with Turgenev and other intellectuals, or the stimulation of the nearby Karlsruhe Opera conducted by his good friend, Levi, it was during his later thirties that Brahms even dallied with the idea of writing an opera. Though it never came to fruition, not even when the perceptive Widmann stepped in with ideas for a libretto, he certainly began to respond to the power of words as never before in his life. A large number of songs, from the *Magelone Romances* to the cycles of Opp. 43, 46, 47, 48 and 49 (including such intimate confessions of love as 'Die Mainacht' and 'Von ewiger Liebe') had emerged in print by 1868. And the *German Requiem* of that year was followed by a sequence of choral works each to an unprecedented degree prompted by personal emotional pressures. The cantata, *Rinaldo* (1863–8), was as far as he felt he could go in appeasing those who wanted something dramatic from him. The *Liebeslieder Waltzes* for voices and piano duet (1868–9) were an outpouring of love for Vienna and all its seductive charms. *The Triumphlied* (1870–1) was a heartfelt patriotic salute to the new, united Germany emerging from war and the defeat of the French: at the outbreak of hostilities he had even briefly considered enlisting.

Still more introspective are the *Schicksalslied* (1868–71) and the *Alto Rhapsody* (1869). It was while staying with his old friend, Dietrich, that early one morning he discovered the Hölderlin poem, contrasting the bliss of Elysium with the heartache of this world, that inspired the *Schicksalslied (Song of Destiny)*. It took hold of him with such force that

9 Extract from the first movement of the G major String Sextet, Op. 36, showing the letters of Agathe's name woven into the texture.

[N.B. In German H = B♮]

even that same day, while on an excursion to the great naval port of Wilhelmshafen which he had asked to see, he wandered off grave and silent from the rest of the group on the beach to start making sketches. For the *Alto Rhapsody*, dedicated to Amalie Joachim, he chose words from Goethe's *Harzreise* ('Winter Journey in the Harz Mountains'), in which a despairing, lonely outcast beseeches divine healing. This work (which he confessed to loving so much that he slept with it under his pillow) grew direct from a brief, intense experience at Lichtental in the early summer of 1869, when he was overcome by the sweet nature of Julie Schumann, Clara's lovely, frail, third daughter, without realizing that she was awaiting a formal offer of marriage from the man she loved, Count Radicati di Marmorito. Clara's diary tells the rest of the story:

> *11th July:* We told our acquaintances of Julie's engagement. Of course I told Johannes first of all; he seemed not to have expected anything of the sort, and to be quite upset. . . .
> *16 July:* Johannes is quite altered, he seldom comes to the house and speaks only in monosyllables when he does come. And he treats even Julie in the same manner, though he always used to be so specially nice to her. Did he really love her? But he has never thought of marrying, and Julie has never had any inclination towards him. . . .
> *End of September (after the wedding):* Johannes brought me a wonderful piece a few days ago, the words from Goethe's *Harzreise*, for alto, male chorus and orchestra. He called it his bridal song. It is long since I remember being so moved by a depth of pain in words and music. . . . This piece seems to me neither more nor less than the expression of his own heart's anguish.

When those words were written in 1869 Brahms was thirty-six and Clara on the verge of fifty. Professional obligations made heavy claims on both, causing many moments of friction. Growing older had not greatly increased Clara's sense of humour or her understanding of Brahms's susceptibility to pretty girls, or his free and easy way with country-folk, innkeepers, and all others prepared to keep him well fed and happy. Brahms in his turn had never developed much tact. A letter to Clara early in 1868, suggesting that rather than continuously complain about the strain of concert tours she should retire, caused almost as much harm (it almost stopped her from going to Bremen for the *German Requiem*) as his remark in Denmark, while on a recital tour with Stockhausen, that Copenhagen's splendid Thorwaldsen Museum was so fine that it ought to be in Berlin. Yet despite all misunderstandings the basic link between them remained unbroken – and both knew it.

Brahms needed this anchorage, for at the end of January 1872 he heard that his father was seriously ill. He had loved him enough to give him unstinted understanding and good wishes when in 1868 he had married Caroline Schnack (a sympathetic, twice-widowed cook who had provided his meals in her eating house after his separation from Christiane), and to invite him on walking tours in the Austrian and Swiss mountains (Jakob had never travelled before) in the summers of 1867 and 1868. Returning to Hamburg in utmost haste, Brahms was granted just a fortnight at the bed-side of this sturdy old journeyman before he eventually died on 11 February of cancer of the liver.

On the Crest of the Wave   VI

Brahms was fond of his stepmother and her son by a former marriage. He always kept in touch with them, and helped them financially. But old ties with Hamburg were loosening. Just before his father's illness he had rented a permanent, furnished apartment in Vienna, at Karlsgasse 4, instead of merely chancing his luck each visit. Subsequently enlarged by the acquisition of a third room to house his ever-growing collection of precious manuscripts, scores and old, rare books, it was the nearest he ever came to a home of his own, and remained his base for life.

Vienna's musical circles were quick to pounce. The moment Anton Rubinstein resigned the conductorship of the renowned Gesellschaft der Musikfreunde, the post was offered to Brahms. Though rather worried about loss of freedom, he did not take long to accept. The salary was generous, and he was allowed a free hand in programme-building and selection of artists. Perhaps he also secretly felt that Hamburg ought to be taught a lesson. His first step was to strengthen the orchestra, bringing it up to a hundred players and replacing amateurs with professionals. Recalling his former struggles with the Singakademie, he also insisted on more rehearsals for the much larger Singverein (some 300 or so voices) which co-operated in each season's six concerts. Older music, especially Bach and Handel, still played a large part in his programmes. But he had learnt that the pleasure-loving Viennese were not antiquarians; he had humour enough to relish a story told against him that 'whenever Herr Brahms was feeling really hilarious, he rushed off to sing "Das Grab ist meine Freude!" ("The grave is my joy")'. In consequence novelties like Max Bruch's *Odysseus*, Goldmark's *Hymn of Spring* and Berlioz's *Harold in Italy* were included besides several of Brahms's own recent choral works; also a good deal of little-known Schubert, Mendelssohn and Schumann. Beethoven's *Missa Solemnis* and

Emperor Concerto, with Brahms himself as solo pianist, were other landmarks. Vienna's musicologists admired his sense of style in old music, notably his insistence on original accompaniments — including harpsichord continuo — rather than refurbishings. The public at large enjoyed his conducting too. One discerning friend specially noted 'your swinging beat, which means so much, your expressive arm movements, which always respond to an impulse from within, and are not merely designed to extract certain results from others, your natural one-ness with the music, which excludes any paltry nervousness as it does deliberately planned effects'. By the end of the third season in the spring of 1875, Brahms was nevertheless very ready to resign from a job wasting too many precious hours in administration. Working at close quarters with an orchestra had rekindled old fires: at this moment all he wanted was time to write orchestral music. Even while in harness he had returned in 1873 to his beloved variation form for a new orchestral set on the old 'Chorale St. Antonii' (introduced by Haydn into his B flat wind *Feldpartita*) making a two-piano version, too, so that his friends could play it at home. But his main objective was the completion of a Symphony in C minor, which had haunted him ever since the Schumann tragedy some twenty years before. He had sent a sketch of the first movement (except for the slow introduction) to Clara as far back as 1862, and for her birthday greeting in September 1868 had quoted the

On the Crest of the Wave

glowing horn theme destined for the finale. 'Thus blew the shepherd's pipe today,' he wrote:

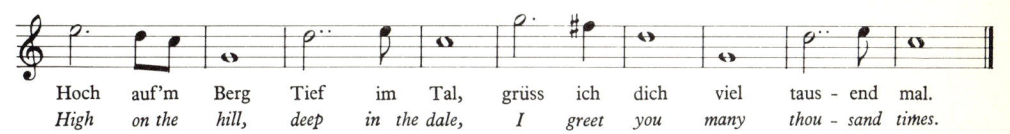

| Hoch | auf'm | Berg | Tief | im | Tal, | grüss | ich | dich | viel | taus - end | mal. |
| High | on the | hill, | deep | in the | dale, | I | greet | you | many | thou - sand | times. |

10 Horn theme from the finale of the C minor Symphony, quoted in 1868 in a letter to Clara.

Yet the world had to wait until November 1876 for the première of the work at Karlsruhe under Dessoff. This was partly because Brahms's self-criticism had intensified a hundred times since the initial failure of his First Piano Concerto. While putting finishing touches to the symphony in the summer of 1876, his holiday companion, the baritone, George Henschel, had invited criticism of some music of his own. 'Go over it again and again until there is not a bar you could improve on,' was Brahms's advice. 'Whether it is beautiful also is an entirely different matter, but perfect it *must* be. You see I'm rather lazy, but I never cool down over a work, once begun, until it is perfected, unassailable.'

Brahms was also more than a little daunted by awareness that in a sense he was taking over the symphonic torch from Beethoven. When eventually reviewing the C minor work, the Viennese critic, Hanslick

Eduard Hanslick

Brahms, Johann Strauss and Hans Richter
(on the wall, Liszt and Wagner)

On the Crest of the Wave

(who only gradually grew to appreciate Brahms's worth) at once commented on an ethical quality in both Beethoven and Brahms not even found in such serious recent symphonists as Mendelssohn and Schumann. And like several other discerning listeners (such as Billroth), Hanslick immediately compared Brahms's struggle for ascendancy over the darker forces of fate in this symphony with Beethoven's in his ninth and last; both works have similar 'joy' themes in their victorious finales.

11 Triumphant main theme from the finale of the C minor Symphony.

On the Crest of the Wave

Supporters of the New German School were quick to deplore Brahms's allegiance to the same kind of orchestra used by Beethoven, without any exotic enlargements such as Wagnerian tubas, also his acceptance of traditional formal procedures – even excluding those experiments in unity and compression through metamorphosis of a 'motto' theme, that obsessed Schumann. But the majority of unprejudiced listeners immediately recognized the symphony as really big music, even if coming from a composer with more to contribute to the sum than to the development of art. Most important of all, Brahms himself was satisfied enough to begin a Second Symphony in D the following year, first performed in Vienna under Richter on 30 December 1877. To Hanslick this was like 'a return to the spring blossoms of earth' after the dark, Faustian struggle of its predecessor. Because so radiant, limpid and lyrical, the new work had an immediate, overwhelming popular success – not least in Holland, where Brahms found himself fêted like a king when he went there to conduct both symphonies early in 1878.

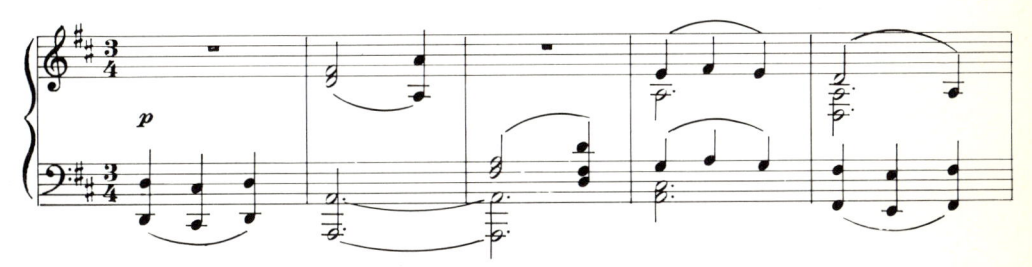

12 Opening of the D major Symphony, embodying Brahms's F A F motto.

Now in his middle forties, Brahms was in fact beginning to understand the true meaning of success. Offers like the Directorship of Music at Düsseldorf, once so coveted, and of the Thomasschule in Leipzig, he could reject, explaining to Billroth (in the context of Düsseldorf) that apart from the obvious advantages of Vienna's wine-houses and refreshments, here 'one can be a bachelor without any more discussion. In a little city, an old bachelor is a caricature.' Because unwilling to make the obligatory personal visit, he also refused an honorary doctorate from Cambridge University. But he was glad to accept the gold medal of London's Philharmonic Society, which could be given *in absentia*, likewise an honorary degree from Breslau University, which he repaid in 1880 with an *Academic Festival Overture* full of exuberant student songs – so exuberant that he quickly followed it up with a *Tragic Overture* to restore the balance. Germany had also made him a Knight of the Order of Maximilian, and even Hamburg, slow to honour its own sons, had invited him as a guest of honour at the fiftieth anniversary celebrations of its Philharmonic Society – an invitation he found it far from easy to fit in amidst the growing demands for his services as conductor or pianist in his own music throughout Europe. At heart, all this official acclaim meant far less to him than a deeply felt word of appreciation from a personal friend, or the compliment of increased brio in the playing of the Hungarian gypsy musicians in the Prater if they caught sight of his now gradually stoutening figure among their listeners. But he was flattered, all the same, and grateful for the income his astute publisher, Simrock, was now reaping from his works, both so as to help the needy (he was as generous to friends as to family) and to indulge his own growing enjoyment of good food, drink, cigars, and last but not least, long sojourns in the country.

Much as Vienna's restaurants, theatres and friendships meant to him, when there was serious composing to be done he felt it imperative to escape – preferably to lakeside villages amidst mountains where he could take long walks and feast his eyes on grand vistas. Choosing each year's spot became a matter of vital importance, the more so since he liked congenial company when each day's work was done. In 1873 it was Tutzing, on the Starnbergersee, where he was ecstatic about the beauty of the lake, even when black after a thunderstorm, against a range of snow-covered mountains. The proximity of friends like Luise Dustmann, the singer, Levi, the conductor, and Allgeyer, the engraver (and biographer of his painter friend, Feuerbach), all added to his pleasure. The following year he chose Rüschlikon, on the lake of Zurich where, besides relishing the fresh-water fish and local wines, he grew very close to the Swiss poet, Widmann. In 1875 he stayed at Ziegelhausen, near Heidelberg, where Feuerbach and 'some charming lady singers from Mannheim' helped to make life 'only too gay', as he put it.

In 1876 it was Sassnitz, on the island of Rügen in the Baltic, which though less comfortable and convenient, he enjoyed for its beauty and equally for a visit from his singer friend, George Henschel. Several times they went swimming, repeatedly diving with eyes wide open for pebbles on the sea bed. Once they made an expedition over the heath in search of Brahms's special bullfrog pond: he loved to catch the tiny frogs, put them on a stone and watch them jump back, convinced from their pathetic bleatings within the interval of a falling diminished third that they were all little fairytale princes and princesses bewitched by wicked magicians. Sometimes he and Henschel merely dozed and reminisced in a large hammock which Henschel slung up in a beechwood, with a view of the sea far below.

In 1877 he discovered Pörtschach, on the Wörthersee, where, in his own words, 'so many melodies fly about that one must be careful not to tread on them'; with sympathetic locals like the doctor and postmistress, and a large, seven-bedded rented house, he liked it enough to go back the next two years too. Close friends even detected its influence on the music he wrote there. 'That symphony is like blue heavens, the murmur of springs, sunshine, and cool green shadows! It must be beautiful at the Wörthersee,' was Billroth's comment on Brahms's No. 2 in D. The Violin Concerto in D, sparked off by Pörtschach in 1878, is in the same mellow, lyrical vein: there is not a trace of bravura just for its own sake. But perhaps in salute to the half-Hungarian Joachim (who helped with details of lay-out in the solo part and wrote a cadenza besides giving the Leipzig première on New Year's Day, 1879), Brahms spiced its finale with more than a few reminders of the Hungarian gypsy style he loved so well.

Apart from their key, there is a further revealing link between the Pörtschach-inspired Second Symphony and Violin Concerto. Much as Brahms liked arpeggio themes for their own sake, it could scarcely have been coincidence that both the horn motif at the start of the Symphony and the opening tune of the Violin Concerto's slow movement surreptitiously embody the notes of his 'happy' F A F motto:

13 Opening theme of the Adagio from the Violin Concerto, embodying Brahms's F A F motto.

In 1880, he moved on to Ischl, where there was sufficient lively company, including Johann Strauss (who had a villa there), to console him for its rain – or at least till he developed a frightening enough attack of aural catarrh, accompanied by deafness, to send him rushing back to Billroth in Vienna.

On the Crest of the Wave

Internationally famous as Billroth had become since his appointment as professor of surgery at the University of Vienna in 1867, he took as personal an interest in Brahms's career as his own. He was the dedicatee, in 1873, of the first two String Quartets (in C minor and A minor, Op. 51) that Brahms decided to publish, after numerous suppressed essays in this medium, and it was in the beautiful music room of Billroth's Viennese home that these and many other new works were tried out for the first time, even if only in keyboard transcription – such as Brahms so often made to please his closest friends. He and Billroth frequently went to the theatre or to an operetta together, followed by an informal late-night meal in one of their favourite little restaurants. And it was Billroth who in the spring of 1878 opened up a whole new world of experience for Brahms by taking him off on holiday to Italy for the first time. Rome came first, where their friend Goldmark was staging his opera, *The Queen of Sheba*, then Naples, Pompeii and Capri. 'I'm often surprised how well prepared he is for Italy, especially for the arts and cultural affairs,' Billroth wrote to his wife. 'He is so full of warm sensitivity for all beauty and in good humour. We do almost everything on foot and find ourselves in splendid shape.' Brahms's enthusiasm reached new peaks on their second trip, with Nottebohm too, in 1881. As Billroth now wrote home, 'Brahms bubbles with desire to speak Italian, has studied grammar for months and learnt all the irregular verbs. However he seldom finds just what he wants for the moment, and looks at me with astonishment when I loose all varieties of words about me.'

Travelling as far south as Sicily on this occasion, Billroth also recognized how deeply affected Brahms was by its breathtaking panoramas. When commenting on the warmly romantic B flat major Piano Concerto that immediately followed this holiday, Billroth at once likened its Adagio to a 'full-moon night in Taormina.'

Another great enrichment of life as he approached his half century was his friendship with Heinrich and Elisabeth von Herzogenberg. Heinrich was director of the Bachverein in Leipzig, and a dedicated, if unremarkable, composer. Before marriage in 1868 Elisabeth had studied piano with Brahms in Vienna, sufficiently disturbing him with her looks, charm and talent for the lessons to be terminated rather abruptly. But with all danger now past, Brahms could happily accept the Herzogenberg's hospitality whenever he passed through Leipzig. He delighted in Elisabeth's splendid cooking. He valued her quick perception and musical judgement, and began to send her new works for comment as often as to Clara Schumann. Perhaps most of all he appreciated her teasing humour (which Clara lacked), and though always a reluctant correspondent, replied to her letters with a far livelier pen than usual. She in her turn was fond enough of him to be able to repay his well-known sarcasm with pointed sallies of her own, to criticize what she considered miscalculations in his music (such as treating voices too much like instruments in some of his songs, now and again at the expense of verbal accentuation – a judgement many other

Elisabeth von Herzogenberg

professional critics have upheld ever since), and last but not least, to protest at certain crudities in his character. His lack of tact when confronted with works by the less talented was notorious. When her husband, Heinrich, was once the victim, in the context of a string quartet, her feelings exploded. 'I know you don't *mean* to be cruel at such times,' she wrote on 10 March 1878. 'It is a kind of 'black dog' (no intimate acquaintance, thank Heaven!) on your back which prompts these speeches, so deadly in their power to wound others. If you knew how deadly, you would give them up; for you are kind enough at bottom, and would never consciously throw scorn on true affection. So do pull up this weed in your garden, and, above all, don't hate me for this interminable letter.'

Clara had also suffered more reminders of Brahms's rougher side: relations between them had been sorely strained during the 1873 Schumann festival at Bonn (to raise funds for a memorial) because of a misunderstanding as to whether Brahms should be represented by his *Requiem* or a new work, resulting in neither. But when the monument was eventually unveiled in 1880 he was a pillar of support with his memorable conducting of Schumann's *Rhenish Symphony* and *Requiem für Mignon*, and no one was more compassionate during dark days of death when in turn Clara lost her father, her daughter Julie, and her son Felix. Perhaps recalling that he had never been closer to Clara than at the time of Felix's birth, he tried to cheer his godson, as his tuberculosis worsened, by setting three of his poems besides enlisting Billroth's medical help. When the end came, his message to Clara in March 1876 was, 'Let this sincere love bring you some comfort. I love you better than anyone or anything in the world.' Opportunities for meeting grew infrequent now that he was constantly on concert travels, and she very much tied to Frankfurt after her appointment in 1878 as principal piano teacher at its Conservatoire. But if needing further proof of his warmth, Clara had only to read between the lines of some of the many songs (including Opp. 63, 69, 70, 71, 72, 84, 85 and 86) composed throughout the 1870s. Brahms was always autobiographical in choice of texts: a song like 'Alte Liebe' ('Old Love') (ending 'dreams of old possess me, and lead me ever back to you') could only have been written with Clara in mind, at a time of need. Into the Op. 85 set he even wove the falling five-note motif that Robert Schumann himself so often used – as at the start of the C major Fantasy for piano – when dreaming of his 'absent beloved'.

Conquests and Conflicts VII

An unforeseen offer from the Meiningen Court Orchestra in the course of 1881 was soon to leave Brahms with even less time for visiting old friends. For years its conductor, Hans von Bülow, had worked unstintingly for Wagner's cause – only to see him elope with his own wife, Cosima. So, needing a new lodestar, he invited Brahms to use Meiningen as a trying-out ground for new works and to join him and the orchestra on their periodic tours so generously encouraged by the Duke to keep spirits fresh. 'An itinerant orchestra, playing not dance music but the greatest works of the symphonic repertory, is a novelty reserved for our railroad epoch,' was Hanslick's comment on the experiment, and Clara Schumann was one of several eminent musicians who at first thought it far beneath Brahms's dignity to throw in his lot with strolling players. But because there was no opera at Meiningen to sap its energy, the orchestra had achieved undreamed of subtleties of ensemble and nuance in the concert repertory under Bülow's baton. Brahms was only too delighted at the prospect of meticulously rehearsed performances of his music reaching a wide audience quickly. Though normally averse to grandees, he also took an instant liking to the natural, cultivated Duke and his wife (formerly a music-loving actress), and gladly accepted their invitations to stay, whether at Meiningen itself, their hunting lodge by the Königssee, or their villa on Lake Como. He even unprotestingly put on formal attire and decorations for their gala receptions – no small concession for one so addicted to shabby old clothes (he once confessed to his friend, Widmann, that one of his reasons for not visiting England was that 'one almost has to live in a dress-suit and white tie').

Meiningen at large immediately recognized the stature of Bülow's new protégé at the introductory concert on 27 November 1881, when the programme included Brahms's C minor Symphony, the *St. Antonii Var-*

Conquests and Conflicts

iations and the *Academic Festival Overture* and *Tragic Overture*, as well as the very recently completed B flat major Piano Concerto, with the composer (who also shared the conducting) as soloist. Eighteen days earlier Brahms had given the official première of the Concerto at Budapest, and by the end of February 1882 had also introduced it to Stuttgart, Zurich, Breslau, Vienna, Leipzig, Hamburg, Berlin, Kiel, Bremen, Münster, Utrecht and Frankfurt, often, though not always, with his new-found colleagues. Not even his staunchest admirers tried to pretend that his piano playing was as reliable as in youth, or that he now looked anything other than middle-aged: he had put on a lot of weight and grown a bushy beard ('a clean-shaven man is taken for an actor or a priest', was his caustic comment). But exept in Leipzig, the Concerto itself (dedicated to his old teacher, Marxsen) was enthusiastically received: after the stark drama of its predecessor in D minor, it struck home as the testimony of a man at peace with himself and the world. The solo part demands a sturdy technique, not least in the high-powered 'Allegro appassionato' which, in defiance of the normal three-movement concerto convention, Brahms introduced for contrast between the opening 'Allegro non troppo' and the Adagio. But again he rejected all Lisztian glitter and exploitation of novel keyboard sonority for its own sake. His prime concern, once more, was to weave piano and orchestra into a close symphonic argument.

At about this time he was sufficiently moved by the death of his old painter friend, Feuerbach, to set Schiller's *Nänie* as a short choral threnody in the classical spirit. This in its turn sparked off the *Gesang der Parzen* ('Song of the Fates'), a dark-textured choral setting of ominous words from Goethe's *Iphigenie*, which he dedicated to the Duke of Meiningen. There were also more chamber works, and new songs inspired by yet another young mezzo-soprano, Hermine Spies, who with her jollity and good-nature, won herself a very warm corner of his heart without demanding anything more. But with Meiningen ready and waiting, it was still the orchestra that lured him most: by the end of the summer of 1883, spent in congenial rented quarters high above Wiesbaden, he had completed a Third Symphony in F.

As Bülow was ill, the première was given in Vienna on 2 December under Hans Richter who, in a toast immediately afterwards, dubbed it Brahms's 'Eroica'. Though Brahms himself, secretive as ever about motivation, would never have admitted it, the nickname was apt. His stoical youthful F A F motto (*frei aber froh*, free but happy) turns up in

14 Opening of the F major Symphony, based on Brahms's F A F motto.

many unexpected places in his works, but nowhere are its implications and connotations more searchingly examined than in this symphony coincidental with his half century. The challenging opening presentation of the motto, with the confident A natural of F major in tug-of-war with the dark A flat of F minor, summarizes the nature of the conflict at once, nor is it conclusively resolved until the very end of the finale, when the symphony's passionate opening theme floats down from the heights in a mood of benign calm. Never was Brahms's orchestration more poetic than in this final coda, once likened to a golden sunset after a stormy day: the seductive string tremolos are almost Wagnerian. The symphony also includes a beautiful, nostalgic example of the lyrical Allegretto-type movement (also found in its two predecessors) that Brahms often preferred to a high-powered Beethovenian Scherzo at this point in his works.

The summers of 1884 and 1885 were both spent at Mürzuschlag, first discovered when walking in the mountains with his father, and close enough to Vienna to permit frequent visits from friends. Here he wrote his fourth and last symphony in E minor, which after thorough rehearsal under Bülow, had its public première under his own baton at Meiningen on 25 October 1885. 'Neither its treasure of ideas nor its chaste beauty is apparent at first glance ... it is like a dark well: the longer we look into it, the more brightly the stars shine back,' was Hanslick's considered verdict. More classically objective than its predecessors, the work ends with a passacaglia movement based on a theme from Bach's 150th cantata, 'Nach dir, Herr, verlanget mich' ('For thee, Lord, do I long') – with one chromatic insertion of Brahms's own as fifth note.* As Schumann had so discerningly observed (see page 26) when Brahms was only twenty, he was not one of those composers, like Beethoven, whose style gradually evolved as the years passed, but

*Marked (x) in Example 15b.

15 Opening theme of the finale from Brahms's E minor Symphony, written as a passacaglia on a theme borrowed from Bach.
a. Bach (Cantata No. 150) **b.** Brahms

rather someone 'springing like Minerva fully armed, from the head of Jove', Nevertheless in this symphony's Bach-inspired finale, Brahms's architectural invention touched its highest peak. Though nothing could shake his belief in the validity of classical tonality, this movement also contains evidence of his increasing awareness of the expressive power of chromaticism: a questing passage such as the lead into the middle section could equally well have come from Liszt or Wagner.

16 Extract from the finale of the E minor Symphony.

Thrilled at an invitation to conduct the work with the Frankfurt Orchestra, Brahms accepted without stopping to think that Bülow and the Meiningen Orchestra were due to perform it in Frankfurt only a few days later. Bülow was hurt enough to resign his appointment and sever all connection with Brahms, to whom he felt he had handed over his baton quite often enough. But Brahms had just fallen out with an earlier champion, Hermann Levi, because of Levi's growing addiction to Wagner: he knew better than to ride a high horse this time. When in Vienna a year or so later, Bülow found Brahms's visiting card pushed under his door with the notes of Pamina's 'Shall I then see thee nevermore?' (from *The Magic Flute*) written on it. The next day the two were again arm-in-arm.

One of the symphony's greatest admirers was Joachim, despite the fact that he, too, had run into personal trouble with its composer. Incensed by Joachim's irrationally excitable suspicions about the relationship of his wife and the publisher, Simrock, Brahms had written Amalie Joachim one of the longest and most explicit letters of his life pledging belief in her innocence – without realizing that it would be read out aloud in the divorce court. To Joachim this smacked of disloyalty. Nevertheless his faith in Brahms's genius remained constant, and he conducted an outstandingly fine performance of the E minor Symphony in Berlin early in 1886. Deeply touched, Brahms now wanted to make a

Conquests and Conflicts

reciprocal gesture. So far his only violin sonata had been Op. 78 in G, of 1879, with a finale incorporating a 'rain' motif (also symbolic of tears) found in two of his songs, 'Regenlied' ('Rain Song') and 'Nachklang' ('Memories'), with words by their mutual poet friend, Klaus Groth. During the summer of 1886 he turned to the violin again, completing a second sonata in A with the word *amabile* at the head of its first movement (it also makes secret cross-references to his song settings of Groth's 'Komm Bald' ('Come Soon') and 'Wie Melodien' ('Fair visions')) besides beginning a third sonata in D minor with as richly nostalgic a slow movement as any to come from his pen.

17 Opening of the finale from the first Violin Sonata in G, Op. 78, its theme borrowed from the earlier song, 'Regenlied'.

18 Brahms's song, 'Regenlied', Op. 59, No. 3.

Wal - le, Re - - - gen, wal - le nie - - der,
Pat - ter, pat - - - ter, rain - drops fal - - ling,

wek - ke mir die Träu - me wie - der,
hap - py child - - hood dreams re - cal - ling,

Conquests and Conflicts

By the summer of 1887 his feelings could no longer be masked: longing for reunion with his old friend overflowed into a double Concerto for Violin and Cello openly declared as being for Joachim and the cellist of his quartet, Robert Hausmann. On 21 September the three artists met at Baden-Baden, where Clara was on holiday, to discuss details of figuration in the solo parts (Joachim favoured more brilliance than Brahms had provided) and to rehearse with the local orchestra in readiness for the official première in Cologne on 18 October, under Brahms's baton. Some listeners were disappointed, considering it too much of a symphony with violin and cello obbligatos, rather than a soloists' concerto. Brahms himself was content. He had written it with his heart's blood, in his own true style, as a work of reconciliation after long misunderstanding: chastened as they were, he knew that Joachim and he could never fall out again. But significantly it was the last time he ever wrote for full orchestra.

The Double Concerto was actually composed at Thun, in the Bernese Oberland, where, beyond the lake, the snow-capped Jungfrau, Eiger and Mönch were constantly in his view. In the summer of 1886 he had rented the first floor of a house just where the river Aar joins the lake, and liking it as much as Pörtschach, returned the next two years. A great deal of his happiness was due to the fact that Joseph Widmann lived at Berne. Every weekend Brahms caught the train from Thun to join this sympathetic writer and his family, including their small daughter, Johanna: he could never resist children, and kept a supply of sweets in his pocket for poor ones. He also had a soft spot for their dog, Argos, whose remarkable, unaided return from the Mer de Glace at Grindelwald, after once getting lost on an excursion, gave the composer just as much of a thrill as any fine performance of his music. Back in Vienna he immediately wrote to enquire: 'How is Argos? Would he take it as a tender greeting from me if you were to give him a nice piece of meat instead of a dog biscuit?'

Always casually dressed, sometimes with an old brown-grey shawl thrown round his shoulders in chilly weather, Brahms usually travelled with a leather satchel stuffed with books borrowed from his host's large library. He was a voracious reader in a variety of spheres, though as in his equally tireless theatre-going, he preferred known and trusted thinkers to the avant-garde. Wherever he was staying he always insisted on getting up early to make his own coffee (a special blend sent by an admirer from Marseilles), and with his zest for excursions and lively interest in everything going on around – from exciting new inventions like the phonogram and electric light to the bears of the Berne zoo, his visits were not exactly regarded by his hosts as days of rest. As Widmann put it, 'the active mind of our guest required a responsive mood in those about him, and everyone was stimulated in the endeavour to keep up to the level of his untiring mental activity.'

Because of Brahms's total unpretentiousness in discussing his own work, Widmann sympathized with his impatience with would-be portrait painters, autograph-hunters and fawners of all kinds, and particularly liked to recount the story of a pedantic Swiss musician, who just having told Brahms he knew every note of his music, suddenly found himself asked by the composer to be quiet as the band was about to play one of his pieces. 'I still seem to see that good man before me,' wrote Widmann, 'as he stood there gaping and listening with upturned eyes to the rather common music (it was a military march by Gingl) which he took for a composition of Brahms, while Brahms himself, in great glee at the success of his ruse, whispered to us, "well fooled".

The house where Brahms stayed near Thun

Conquests and Conflicts

But like Elisabeth von Herzogenberg, Widmann once or twice had cause to deplore Brahms's caustic mirth at the expense of less talented composers, especially those who treated their own meagre efforts too reverentially. More than once Widmann also suffered from Brahms's dogmatic arrogance when stating a point of view, not least in matters of nationalist (he was an ardent patriot) or political import: an argument over monarchial and republican forms of government, with Widmann strong in support of the latter, once almost cost them their friendship. Yet like others closest to Brahms, Widmann knew that the rough had to be taken with the smooth for the sake of the rock-like integrity beneath. He knew that if any friend or colleague ever really fell on hard times, Brahms never failed – as the musicologists, Nottebohm and Pohl, both discovered in terminal illness.

Towards the end of 1888 Brahms even persuaded Clara to accept a gift of 10,000 marks refused earlier in the year. At sixty-nine she was wracked with sorrow and anxiety about her children and grandchildren (her third son, Ferdinand, was now critically ill), while her own deteriorating health, particularly the neuralgia in her arm, was compelling her to cancel far more concerts than she could afford. No doubt Brahms had Clara in mind when, instead of producing more of those big, arduous sonatas and sets of variations of former days, he now wrote only intimate miniatures for the piano. Nevertheless the fourteen-year gap between them was beginning to take its toll. Sometimes disagreements were only superficial, and quickly appeased in music-making together, especially if in the company of any of her pupils. Other quarrels were serious. She was incensed by his determination to publish the original version of her husband's D minor Symphony, which he preferred to the heavily scored revision; he in his turn was put out because the complete Breitkopf edition of Schumann edited by Clara omitted certain unpublished juvenilia which he particularly admired (they eventually appeared in a supplementary volume).

What probably piqued Clara most of all was the knowledge that Brahms's own new works, previously always sent off to her at once for criticism, now went first to Billroth, or more often still, to Elisabeth von Herzogenberg. Even Brahms recognized the danger. In one letter to Elisabeth he begged her to forward a manuscript speedily, 'because Frau Schumann is very touchy'. The sensitive Herzogenbergs always understood. In their great goodwill and devotion to both great artists, they even invited Clara to stay with them in Nice and Florence during

Heinrich's convalescence after a long illness, and loved having her. But as they wrote to Brahms in May 1889:

> we wish she could enjoy all the beauties of the place at the cost of less exertion. The dear thing has ten years too many on her shoulders, and has not the elasticity of temperament which one must possess if one would be perfectly happy among the Italians in spite of the dirt, fraud and general discomfort . . . once or twice we found her miserably seated on her camp-stool before some Signorelli or Verocchio, rubbing her hands nervously and trying so hard to feel some enthusiasm. But nothing would come and carry her off her feet.

'I was right not to attempt it,' Brahms wrote back, perhaps secretly guilty that in his own desire always to be on the move so as to see as much as possible, he had never arranged an Italian rendezvous with Clara himself. But 'the pathetic side of it', as he put it in the same letter, plainly pained him.

Despite passing shadows, life was good for Brahms as he advanced into his fifties. In 1889 he was awarded the Order of Leopold by the Austrian Emperor. More important still, he was given the Honorary Freedom of his native city of Hamburg – pleasing him enough to forget past slights, to go there in person for its Industrial and Commercial Exhibition, and to dedicate a new, patriotic eight-part motet, *Fest-und Gedenksprüche* ('Festival and Commemoration Pieces'), to the Burgomaster. In Vienna, a splendid new housekeeper called Frau Truxa eased many domestic problems: she was the widow of a writer, and Brahms became very fond of her two children. For summer escape he deserted Thun, from 1889 onwards, for his old favourite, Ischl; its nearness to Vienna and all his friends increasingly outweighed his dislike of its rainfall. Last but not least, there was always Italy to explore in the spring if congenial travelling companions could be found – and Widmann was now one of his favourites. Their first trip together in 1888 included Bologna, where they visited an international exhibition of old manuscripts (always of enormous interest to Brahms) and had a most enjoyable encounter with the town's music director-composer, Giuseppe Martucci. They also visited Loreto, where Brahms was shattered by the contrast between the ecstatic devotion of a vast crowd of pilgrims, who had dragged themselves on their knees to the sanctuary, and the almost contemptuous attitude of the priests. In Rome they made several excursions (usually on foot) in memory of Feuerbach, who once lived there.

The house where Brahms stayed in Ischl

Italian opera lured them not at all. But finding themselves alone in the carriage as their train passed through Pesaro, each in turn sang an aria from *The Barber of Seville* in salute to Rossini.

Returning to Northern Italy together in 1890, Brahms was profoundly moved by Parmigiano's painting, *Bethrothal of St. Catherine*, at Parma, and scarcely less by the Cathedral at Cremona in the moonlight. One of his happiest discoveries in Cremona was nevertheless a statue of St. Joachim. It tickled him vastly that his old friend should have a saintly namesake in this 'venerable old city of violins'.

The mature celebrity

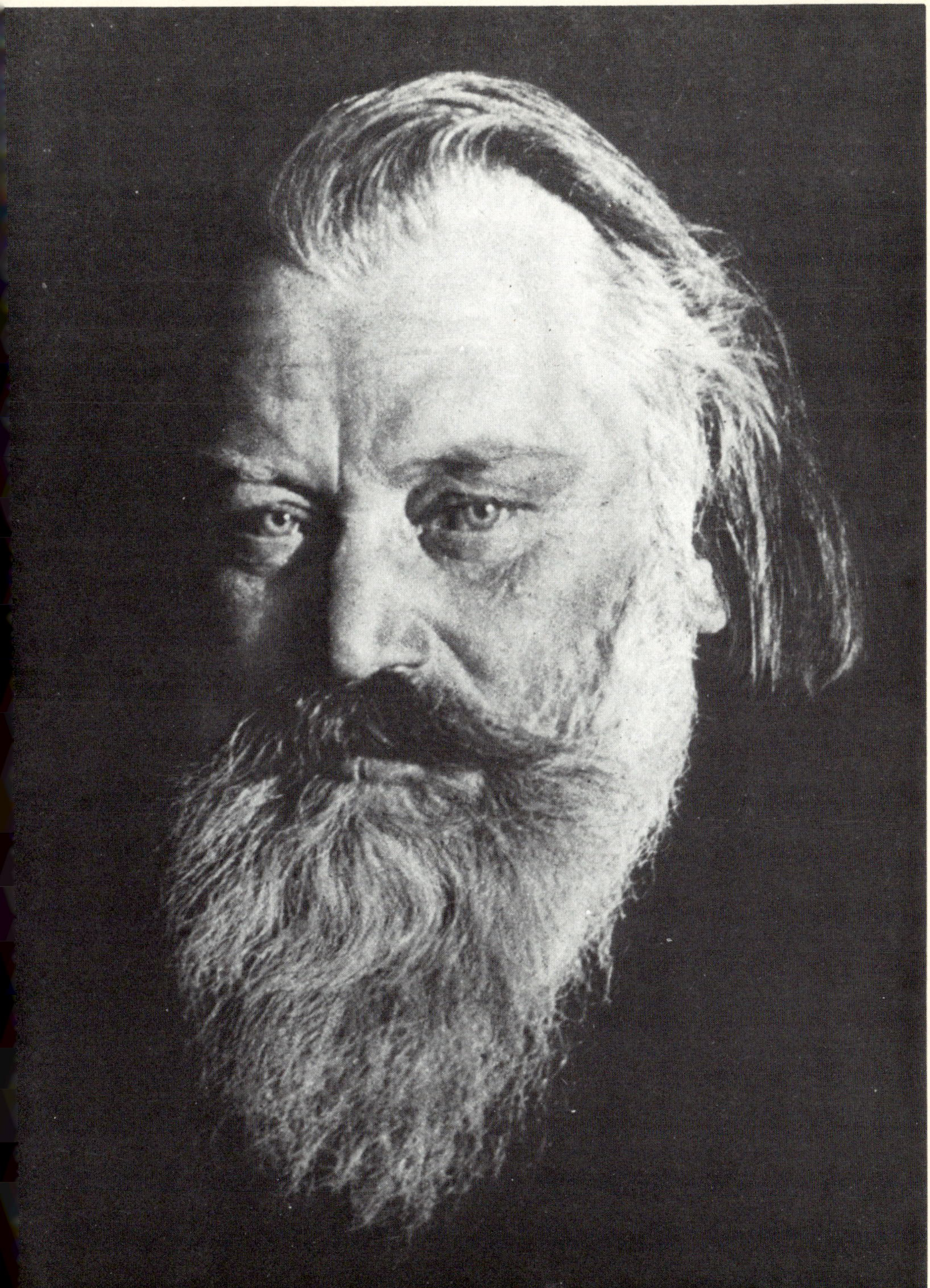

VIII   Approaching the End

In the spring of 1893 Brahms set out for Italy for the eighth (and last) time. Sad as he was at missing his 'asparagus' birthday lunch (organised annually by the Viennese piano representative, Friedrich Ehrbar, always with asparagus as the special treat, for a dozen or so close friends), he was all too keenly aware that this May he would be sixty, that the Vienna Gesellschaft der Musikfreunde was striking a special medal of him for the occasion, and that there would be no end to the official deputations and receptions unless he made his escape. Widmann was again his mainstay, and they were joined by the Swiss conductor, Friedrich Hegar, and the Hungarian-Swiss pianist, Robert Freund, with Sicily as the goal.

'Though according to the *Winter's Tale* the Bohemians are a seafaring nation, this assertion has not yet been made with regard to the Hungarians', was Brahms's quip to Freund when, on arriving at Genoa, they found the only available ship was Hungarian. Disliking sea-travel, he was ready to jump at any excuse for going by train to Naples, where they broke their journey to visit Hanslick and his wife on holiday at Sorrento. Sitting amidst orange-trees in the sun, watching dolphins playing in the blue bay of Naples below, someone proposed champagne to seal the joy of the hour. Brahms's immediate reaction was to seize hold of the large chianti flask on the table, protesting that in such surroundings any other drink was unthinkable. Hanslick rose to the occasion. 'At last I have important news for the musical world,' he remarked: 'Gran fiasco di Brahms!' ('Brahms's great fiasco!').

In Naples, Brahms did allow himself to be lured aboard an Italian boat for Palermo: the night was calm, and he spent most of it on deck watching the phosphorescent ripples in their wake, and then a glorious sunrise. It was twelve years since his previous visit to Sicily with

Brahms in 1893, characteristically striding with hands behind back

Brahms on his way to 'The Red Hedgehog'

Billroth, but no intervening discoveries in any way diminished his spontaneous delight in its gaily decorated horses and carts, its natural beauty, or its ruins – this time Girgenti, Catania, Syracuse and Taormina were the main centres of exploration. Though nine years younger, Widmann was often exhausted by Brahms's constant activity: even on holiday he always rose at 5.00 a.m. But they were at one in liking to do as much as possible on foot, and in preferring simple inns to sophisticated hotels. Unlike several other friends, Widmann was never even known to complain of Brahms's snoring – sometimes quite loud enough to penetrate thin walls. They were back in Naples by 7 May for the great day itself: while Hegar and Freund went off to explore Pompeii, Brahms spent the greater part of his sixtieth birthday at the bedside of the incapacitated Widmann who had broken an ankle as they boarded ship. But their likely arrival time and address had somehow leaked back home. Congratulatory telegrams poured in all day. One from the teaching staff of the Vienna Conservatoire congratulated him on reaching the age of seventy. 'Not accepted. I protest,' was his joking reply on returning it.

Approaching the End

Back in Vienna, there was one big difference in the pattern of his life: at sixty he no longer wanted so strenuous a round of travel as conductor or pianist in his own works throughout each 'Conzertwinter', as he called it. An invitation in 1894 to become permanent conductor of the Hamburg Philharmonic Society occasioned his most ironic refusal of all:

> There are not many things that I have desired so long and so ardently at the time – that is at the right time. Many years had to pass before I could reconcile myself to the thought of being forced to tread other paths. Had things gone according to my wish, I might today be celebrating my jubilee with you, while you would be, as you are today, looking for a capable younger man. May you find him soon, and may he work in your interests with the same goodwill, the same modest degree of ability, and the same whole-hearted zeal, as would have done yours very sincerely, J. Brahms.

Financially, Brahms could afford to pick and choose: Simrock's business acumen had made him wealthy. But though as generous to deserving friends and causes as to his stepmother, his only personal luxury, as always, was the purchase of musical manuscripts and rare books. For the rest he preferred the simple life he had always known. The proximity of Frau Truxa and her two boys helped to warm his flat, and he never

Brahms at Gmunden with the daughters of a friend

Brahms with Johann Strauss in Ischl

Approaching the End

missed Christmas Eve present-giving with them around a lighted tree. For regular meals he went to The Red Hedgehog: knowing his own prickly reputation the name attracted him as much as the cooking. But he preferred the privacy of a small, dark, back room to the smarter main restaurant, and though relishing his food and drink never ordered extravagantly.

Life at Ischl, now his regular summer retreat, was just as unpretentious. Liking his simple landlord and wife, he always took the first floor of a small house built on a mountain slope overlooking the river on the outskirts of the resort. He usually ate at the Hotel Kaiserin Elisabeth, characteristically in its cheaper, less formal underground 'Keller', before going on to Walter's coffee-house to read the papers, and then to visit friends. Ischl's main attraction for him still lay in the congenial company it offered. It was near for visitors from Vienna. An hour's journey by train or boat took him to Billroth's lakeside retreat at St. Gilgen, and it was just as easy to get to other close friends at Gmunden. Walking in the mountains was still his favourite relaxation, though with growing corpulence he could only keep up his notoriously vigorous step when coming downhill. Even on weekend excursions into the gentler countryside around Vienna with members of the Tonkünstlerverein, a music society of which he was elected honorary president in

1886, he now often got out of breath. When suddenly commanded to stop and admire the view, his perceptive younger friends, including the librarian of the Gesellschaft der Musikfreunde, Eusebius Mandyczewski, of whom Brahms was particularly fond, immediately obliged at length since they knew what this really meant.

Despite rival factions in the Austrian capital (notably those of Bruckner and Hugo Wolf) it was Brahms that every visiting musician of note first wanted to meet and every music-loving family to entertain: not surprisingly, lionization brought its dangers. Though usually angelic with true friends such as Dr. Fellinger and his sculptress wife (with whom he always spent Christmas Day), Brahms could also behave like a spoilt child. He grew to expect his favourite dishes. Once an entire table had to be relaid because he wanted to eat outside on the balcony. More and more, too, he showed his dislike of contradiction when expressing opinions. Yet modesty over his own compositions disarmed everyone. He frequently horrified Elisabeth von Herzogenberg by posting precious manuscripts, unregistered, in old wrappers tied up with string. Any well-meaning attempt to equate him with the great was invariably dismissed with a joke. Once when he and Henschel were invited to lunch by an eminent wine-merchant in Koblenz, a splendid old bottle of Rauenthaler '65 was reverentially opened at the end of the meal. 'Yes gentlemen, what Brahms is among composers, this Rauenthaler is among wines,' said their host. 'Then let's have a bottle of Bach now,' was Brahms's quick retort. It was veneration for Bach that once prompted him, as a sexagenarian, to make an unusually personal confession to the director of Breitkopf und Härtel, currently publishing the Leipzig Bach Gesellschaft. 'Every man has a few experiences which cause him to feel that his life has been worth living', he wrote. 'For myself I can mention three: that I knew Schumann when I was young; that it was my fortune to live through the year 1870*; and that I have been privileged to watch the constantly increasing glorification of Bach during the past years through the means of your edition.'

Modesty notwithstanding, he was enormously gratified at the rapturous reception he was given in Leipzig in January, 1895, when one of the three programmes of his works included the D minor Piano Concerto once hissed at the Gewandhaus. Nor was he unaware of the honour Meiningen did him that September by coupling him with Bach and Beethoven in a weekend festival dedicated to the 'three Bs'. Shortly afterwards, when invited to conduct his *Triumphlied* at the opening of

*See page 57

Approaching the End

Zurich's new concert hall, he was no less moved to see his own portrait painted on the ceiling alongside heroes like Beethoven and Mozart – though at the party afterwards he typically chose the company of his host's attractive young daughter and her friends, serving a favourite Swiss wine called 'Sauser' at an improvised buffet on the stairs, to that of official guests. A bequest of £1,000 from a totally unknown Englishman, Adolph Behrens, in gratitude for musical pleasure, also touched him deeply: he donated it anonymously to various musical charities.

Many friends still confidently anticipated big new works. Grieg, an enthusiastic visitor to Vienna, even tried to lure him to Norway with hints that in its awe-inspiring landscape, 'the treasure – your fifth symphony – lies hidden!' But as in his concert activities, so in his music Brahms was beginning to withdraw. Chamber music, keyboard miniatures and songs seemed a far more suitable medium for the intimate sentiment he now wanted to express.

After the marriage of Hermine Spies, another seductive-toned mezzo-soprano called Alice Barbi stepped into his life to fan his interest in song. At the time of his sixtieth birthday it was nevertheless folk-song rather than Lieder that claimed him: as a life-long collector, in 1894 he published his forty-nine favourites with piano accompaniments of his own. 'The snake bites its own tail' he wrote to a friend, in reference to the fact that for the last song he chose 'Verstohlen geht der Mond auf' ('The moon steals up'), used as the theme of the variation movement in his C major Piano Sonata, Op.1.

Brahms and the Beggar

Approaching the End

In the sphere of chamber music it was Richard Mühlfeld, clarinettist of the Meiningen Orchestra, who chiefly rekindled his imagination: the clarinet trio and quintet of 1891, like the two clarinet sonatas of 1894, were all inspired by the instrument's capacity for nostalgic romance as revealed by this super-sensitive artist. Whereas his G major String Quintet of 1890 had been spring-like enough for someone to nickname it 'Brahms on the Prater', the mood of the clarinet quintet was autumnal. As he wrote it, his radiantly teasing, upbraiding, loving Elisabeth von Herzogenberg (who had first enthused to him about Mühlfeld in a letter as early as 1882) was seriously ill with a heart disease. Early in January 1892 she died. 'I am too much with you in thought to be able to write. . . . You know how unutterably I myself suffer by the loss of your beloved wife, and can gauge accordingly my emotions in thinking of you, who were associated with her by the closest possible of ties,' was how Brahms, far more easily able to put feelings into music than words, struggled to comfort her husband.

Nor was Elisabeth his only grief: his sister, Elise, the singer Hermine Spies (his dear 'Herminchen'), and Philippine, the wife of his old friend, Otto Grimm, all died within the next few years. Among his men friends, the toll was yet worse. 1894 was the blackest year of all, robbing him of his champion, Hans von Bülow, and more personally, of Billroth. Though growing temperamental differences between them had been exacerbated at the end by a book on musical aesthetics that Billroth was writing, which Brahms plainly considered outside a surgeon's province, basic affection had remained true and deep. Brahms's sense of loss was sharp. 'We are in the front line now, Herr Grüber,' he remarked grimly to his Ischl landlord.

Awareness of life's transience coloured his piano music, too. The publication of a collection of 51 Exercises in 1893 showed how much he still recognized the value of a strong technique. But his own personal emotion found outlet in groups of introspective, chromatically intensified miniatures, more often than not called Intermezzos, which, simple as they were to play, seemed to spring from deeper places of the heart than anything he had previously written for the keyboard. What they meant to Clara, now too frail to play outside her own personal circle of friends and pupils, gave him the greatest satisfaction of all in composing them. 'It really is marvellous how things pour from him . . . it is wonderful how he combines passion and tenderness in the smallest of spaces,' she confided to her diary of the pieces eventually published as his Op. 118 and Op. 119.

19 The opening of the Intermezzo in E flat major, Op. 117, No. 2.

Approaching the End

In their private relationship, an exchange of letters at the time of Clara's 73rd birthday in 1892 had miraculously eased the tensions recently threatening a life-time's devotion. 'You and your husband are to me the best experience of my life, and represent its greatest riches and the noblest that it contains,' were some of his own words. Opportunities for meeting were rarer than ever, but whenever near Frankfurt Brahms stayed at her house as happily as of old. But a visit on his way back from Meiningen in 1895 opened his eyes to her fast deteriorating health. When news of a stroke reached their circle of friends in March 1896, Brahms tried to prepare himself for the inevitable. As he put it in a letter to Joachim:

> The idea of losing her cannot frighten us any more, not even my lonely self, for whom there are far too few living in this world. And when she has gone from us, will not our faces light up with joy at the remembrance of her, of this glorious woman, whose great qualities we have been permitted to enjoy through a long life, only to love and admire her more and more? In this way only shall we grieve for her.

Again music began to stir in him almost without his own volition, this

Brahms at Ischl in 1896

Brahms at the wedding anniversary of his friend the Fellingers, 15 June 189

Approaching the End

time the *Four Serious Songs* for bass and piano, with words from the Bible (as previously in the *Requiem*) seeking comfort for death's sting not so much in the Christian concept of resurrection as belief in the sovereignty of love. The songs were finished by his own 63rd birthday on 7 May 1896, an occasion made the more poignant by a scarcely intelligible greeting from Clara herself, who ever since their first meeting, had never forgotten this anniversary. Only thirteen days later she was dead.

In his distress he took the wrong train, arriving in Frankfurt too late for the funeral service, and only just getting to Bonn in time to throw a handful of earth on to Clara's coffin as it was lowered into the ground alongside her husband. Forty hours of continuous travel on top of such emotional strain totally exhausted him; back in Ischl all his friends at first attributed his sallow complexion, loss of weight and reduced vitality in the next few weeks to this alone. He himself again turned to composition for relief, and by Midsummer's Day had completed a set of eleven Bach-inspired chorale-preludes for organ. Since he had always used music as a kind of diary of his own innermost experience, it did not escape the attention of those closest to him that for the last he had chosen the chorale 'O Welt ich muss dich lassen' ('O World, I must depart from thee').

20 Brahms's last composition, from the Eleven Chorale Preludes for organ, 'O World, I must depart from thee'.

da - zu mein Leib und
com - mit my soul and
pp
f
Le - - ben
bo - - dy
be-
Un-
p
pp
f
-fehl'n in Got - tes gnäd' - - - - - - ge Hand.
- to the Lord's all lov - - - - - ing hands.
p
pp

Approaching the End

Though despising sickness all his life, he now felt sufficiently unwell to let himself be persuaded to call the Ischl doctor. Jaundice was diagnosed and reluctantly he went off to Karlsbad, as ordered, for a three weeks' course of its remedial salts and waters. But when Viennese and Karlsbad specialists examined him, they at once recognized the truth: like his father, he had cancer of the liver.

Brahms had let it be known that he never wanted to be told 'anything unpleasant', and on returning to Vienna in early October, stoically pretended that nothing was wrong. But his shrinking frame and unhealthy colour betrayed the worst even to those not let into the secret: there were few days throughout the winter when he was without invitations to the homes of personal friends, or kind gestures from countless others outside Vienna. When the wife of the Duke of Meiningen sent him some slippers she had made herself, she even enclosed a stamped addressed postcard that he could return rather than waste energy on a formal acknowledgement.

Two visits from Joachim and his quartet brought him particular pleasure: at their second concert in early January Brahms's G major String Quintet was so warmly applauded that there were tears in his eyes when, at Joachim's insistence, he came on to the platform. There were still more moving scenes at the Philharmonic concert on 7 March. Vienna's music-lovers now sensed that time was running out. From his customary seat in the director's box he was four times called to his feet to acknowledge tumultuous applause at the end of each movement of his E minor Symphony. Again he had to choke back tears. The occasion meant all the more to him in that the programme also included the Cello Concerto of Dvořák, a composer he had always gone out of his way to encourage and help. Earlier that year, when playing through the work at home with Hausmann, enthusiasm for it was enough to make him exclaim, 'Had I known that such a cello concert could be written, I would have tried to compose one myself.'

On 13 March he struggled out into public once more for the première of the operetta, *Die Göttin der Vernunft* ('The Goddess of Reason'), by his old friend, Johann Strauss, but was obliged to let himself be taken home by cab at the end of the second act. By 26 March he was even too weak to get out of bed. With Frau Truxa nearby, he died early in the morning of 3 April, 1897.

Flowers piled up in his room almost hiding the coffin from sight. The funeral procession itself, escorted by riders in old Spanish costume on

Approaching the End

coal-black horses, included as many as six open carriages loaded with floral tributes from musicians all over Europe. A pause was made outside the building of the Gesellschaft der Musikfreunde, imposingly draped in black cloth, with subdued flames burning from high open bowls each side of the door, so that members of the Singverein could sing his own 'Fahr wohl'. There was more music at the old church in the Dorothëer Gasse, and one last choral song at the grave – close to those of Beethoven and Schubert, and the monument to Mozart.

Meanwhile in Hamburg, ships in the harbour flew their flags at half-mast. That might have pleased Brahms most of all.

Suggestions for Further Reading

Brahms: His Life and Work (London 1936, second ed. 1948) by Karl Geiringer is the most comprehensive recent survey, both biographical and musical, in the English language, but Peter Latham's *Brahms* in the Master Musicians series (London 1948) is a compact and easily available purchase. Florence May's lengthy, detailed *Life of Johannes Brahms* (2 vols., London 1905, new ed. 1948) has the invaluable interest of having been written by someone who once had piano lessons from Brahms, and knew him and many of his friends personally. For insight into Brahms's relationship with Clara Schumann Berthold Litzmann's *Clara Schumann: An Artist's Life* (abridged and translated by G. E. Hadow, London 1913) includes many revealing diary entries and extracts from letters. There are also English translations of Brahms's correspondence with his friends, Elisabeth and Heinrich von Herzogenberg, *Johannes Brahms: The Herzogenberg Correspondence* (ed. Max Kalbeck, trans. Hannah Bryant, London 1909), and of his correspondence with the great surgeon, Theodor Billroth, *Johannes Brahms and Theodor Billroth, Letters from a Musical Friendship* (ed. H. Barkan, Norman, Oklahoma, 1957), offering a close-up view of the composer as a man and working musician. Other first-hand glimpses of Brahms can be found in memoirs and monographs by Albert Dietrich and Joseph Widmann, *Recollections of Johannes Brahms* (trans. Dora Hecht, London 1899), George Henschel, *Personal Recollections of Johannes Brahms* (Boston, Mass., 1907), Ethel Smyth, *Impressions that Remained* (London 1919) and Adelina de Lara, *Finale* (London 1955). But a word of warning is obligatory: as most of these older books are out of print, they will have to be tracked down in antiquarian bookshops or music libraries.

Summary of Brahms's Works

Orchestral
Four Symphonies, in C minor, D major, F major and E minor
Two Piano Concertos, in D minor and B flat major
Violin Concerto in D major
Double Concerto in A minor for violin and cello
Two Overtures ('Tragic' and 'Academic Festival')
Variations on the St. Antonii Chorale
Two Serenades, in D major and A major

Choral
A German Requiem
Alto Rhapsody
Schicksalslied (Song of Destiny)
Triumphlied (Song of Triumph)
Liebeslieder Waltzes (two sets)
Nänie
Gesang der Parzen (Song of the Fates)
   A very large number of shorter part-songs, with and without accompaniment

Chamber
Three Violin and Piano Sonatas, in G major, A major and D minor
Two Cello and Piano Sonatas, in E minor and F major
Two Clarinet (or Viola) and Piano Sonatas, in F minor and E flat major
Three Piano Trios, in B major, C major and C minor
Trio for violin, horn and piano in E flat major

Summary of Brahms's Works

Trio for clarinet, cello and piano in A minor
Three Piano Quartets, in G minor, A major and C minor
Three String Quartets, in C minor, A minor and B flat major
Two String Quintets, in F major and G major
Piano Quintet in F minor
Quintet for clarinet and strings in B minor
Two String Sextets, in B flat major and G major

Piano
Three Piano Sonatas, in C major, F sharp minor and F minor
Variations on a theme by Schumann
Variations on an original theme
Variations on a Hungarian theme
Variations on a theme by Paganini
Variations on a theme by Schumann (piano duet)
Variations on the St. Antonii Chorale (two pianos)
Hungarian Dances (piano duet)
   A large number of shorter Intermezzos, Cappriccios, Rhapsodies, Ballades and Romances, grouped in six sets as Opp. 76, 79, 116, 117, 118 and 119

Organ
Eleven Chorale Preludes

Vocal
   Over 200 songs, also a very large number of folk-song arrangements

ACKNOWLEDGEMENTS
The illustrations on pp. 8, 15, 16, 21 (right), 30, 33, 36 (all), 63, 78, 82, 83, 85 (all), 86, 87, 92 and 93 are reproduced by kind permission of Gesellschaft der Musikfreunde, Vienna; that on p. 11 is reproduced by kind permission of Museum der Stadt, Gmunden; that on p. 21 (left) by kind permission of Bibliothèque Inguimbertine, Carpentras; those on pp. 39, 53 and 55 by kind permission of the Österreichische Nationalbibliothek, Vienna. The illustration on p. 44 is taken from E. Michelmann's *Agathe von Siebold*, Göttingen, 1930.

Index

Allgeyer, Julius, 66
Arnim, Bettina von, 23
Arnim, Gisela von, 23, 29

Bach, J. S., 33, 48, 54, 61, 74, 88
Baden-Baden, 54, 55, 78
Barbi, Alice, 89
Bargheer, Karl, 38
Beethoven, Ludwig van, 11, 12, 23, 32, 33, 35, 37, 44, 45, 61, 63, 64, 65, 74, 88, 89, 97
Behrens, Adolph, 89
Berlin *Echo*, 46
Berlioz, Hector, 27, 61
Billroth, Theodor, 54, 64, 65, 67–8, 85, 87, 90
Blume, Herr, 17, 22, 30
Bocklet, Carl Maria von, 12
Bonn, 70
Brahms family:
  Caroline, *née* Schnack (stepmother), 60, 61
  Christiane (mother), 9–10, 20–1, 22, 49, 60
  Elise (sister), 9, 13, 34, 49
  Fritz (brother), 9, 14, 49
  Jakob (father), 9–11, 39, 49, 60
Brahms, Johannes, works of:
Orchestral:
Double Concerto in A minor for violin and cello, 78–9
Overtures: 'Academic Festival' and 'Tragic', 66, 72
Piano Concertos: D minor, 35–6, 43, 51, 63, 88; B flat major, 68, 72
Serenades in D major and A major, 38, 48
Symphonies: C minor, 36, 62–4, 71, 99; D major, 65, 67, 99; F major, 72, 73, 99; E minor, 74, 75, 96
Variations on the St. Antonii Chorale, 62, 71–2
Violin Concerto in D major, 67

Choral:
Alto Rhapsody, 57, 59
Fest-und Gedenksprüche (Festival and Commemoration Pieces), 81
German Requiem, 45, 49–54, 57, 59, 70, 93
Gesang der Parzen (Song of the Fates), 72
Liebeslieder Waltzes, 57
Nänie, 72
Rinaldo, 57
Schicksalslied (Song of Destiny), 57–9
Triumphlied (Song of Triumph), 57, 88–9

Chamber:
Cello Sonata in E minor, 57
Clarinet Quintet, 90
Clarinet Sonatas, 90
Clarinet Trio and Quintet, 90
Fantasy Trio for piano, violin and cello, 23
Horn Trio, 57
Piano Quartets: C minor, 36, 100; G minor, 48; A major, 48
Piano Quintet in F minor, 57
Piano Trio in B major, 28

101

Index

Scherzo in C minor for a Sonata for violin and piano, written jointly with Schumann and Albert Dietrich, 25–6, 27
String Quartets: C minor, 68; A minor, 68
String Quintet in G major, 90, 96
String Sextet in G major, 57, 58
Violin Sonata in A, 76
Violin Sonata in D minor, 76
Violin Sonata in G, 76

Piano:
Ballades, 35
Fifty-one Exercises, 90
Hungarian Dances, 16, 57
Intermezzos, 90, 91
Scherzo in E flat minor, 18, 19, 20
Sonatas: C major, 18, 23, 25, 27, 89; F sharp minor, 18, 24; F minor, 25, 31
Variations on a theme by Handel, 48
Variations on a theme by Paganini, 57
Variations on a theme by Schumann, 31, 32, 35
Variations on the St. Antonii Chorale, 62
Waltz in E major, 56

Organ:
Chorale Preludes, 93, 94

Vocal:
Four Serious Songs, 92–3
'Komm Bold', 76
'Liebestreu', 18
Magelone Romances, 12, 57
Marienlieder, 38
'Regenlied', 76, 77
Song-cycles of Opp. 14 and 19, 43
Song-cycles of Opp. 43, 46, 47, 48 and 49, 57
'Wie Melodien', 76
'Wiegenlied', 40–1

Breitkopf und Härtel, 26–7, 80, 88
Bremen, 33
Brendel, Franz, 45, 46
Bruch, Max, 61
Bruckner, Anton, 88
Bülow, Hans von, 28, 71, 72, 75, 90

Chopin, Frédéric, 12, 37
Cologne, 32, 35
Cornelius, Peter, 20, 47
Cossel, Friedrich Wilhelm, 10, 11
Cranz, August (publisher), 14
Czerny, Carl, 54

Danzig, 33
Deichmann Family, 22
Dessoff, Felix Otto, 63
Detmold, 37–9
Detmold, Prince Leopold III and Princess Friederike, 37–9
Dietrich, Albert, 24, 25, 34, 39, 42, 43, 46, 57
Dusseldorf, 22, 23, 29, 31, 32, 33, 34, 35, 37, 43, 65
Dustman, Luise, 66
Dvořák, Antonin, 96

Endenich asylum, 29, 32
Ehrbar, Friedrich, 84

Faber, Frau (Bertha Porubszky), 41
FAE (Joachim's motto), 25

Index

FAF, Brahms's motto, 25, 65, 67, 72, 73
Fellinger, Richard, 88
Feuerbach, Anselm, 66, 72, 81
Frankfurt, 70, 72, 92, 93
Frankfurt Orchestra, 75
Freund, Robert, 84

Geiringer, Karl, 47
Gesellschaft der Musikfreunde, 61, 84, 88, 97
Giesemann, Adolph, 12, 17
Giesemann, Lieschen, 12–13, 17, 21
Goethe, Johann Wolfgang von, 45, 54, 59, 72
Goldmark, Karl, 61, 68
Gottingen, 20, 24, 42, 43
Grieg, Edvard, 89
Grimm, Julius Otto, 28, 29, 42, 43, 46, 90
Grimm, Philippine, 42, 90
Groth, Klaus, 76
Grund, Friedrich, 46

Hamburg, 9ff., 13ff., 27, 31, 33, 34, 37, 60, 72, 81
Hamburg Ladies' Choir, 40–2
Hamburg Philharmonic Society, 86
Hamm, 39, 42
Handel, George Frideric, 61
Hanover, 18, 28
Hanslick, Eduard, 63–4, 65, 71, 84
Härtel, Dr., 27; *see also* Breitkopf und Härtel
Hausmann, Robert, 78
Haydn, Joseph, 12, 38, 44, 62
Hegar, Friedrich, 84
Hellmesberger Quartet, 48
Henschel, George, 54, 63, 66–7, 88

Herzogenberg, Elisabeth von, 68–70, 80–1, 88, 90
Herzogenberg, Heinrich, 68–70
Hiller, Ferdinand, 22
Hoffmann, E. T. A., 10, 22, 29, 30

Ischl, 67, 87, 93, 96
Italy, 68, 81–2, 84–5

Japha, Louise, 14, 22, 23
Joachim, Amalie, *see* Weiss, Amalie
Joachim, Joseph, 18, 20–2, 23, 24, 25, 26, 28, 29, 32, 33, 34, 38, 39, 40, 42, 44, 45, 48, 67, 75, 78, 92, 96

Karlsbad, 96
Karlsruhe, 55, 57, 63
Kiel, Kappellmeister, 37, 39
Kreisler, Johannes junior (Brahms's pseudonym), 10, 40

Leipzig, 33, 34, 44, 45, 65, 68, 72, 88
Levi, Hermann, 45, 57, 66, 75
Liszt, Franz, 18, 20, 27, 45, 46, 75
Loreto, 81

Mandyczewski, Eusebius, 88
Marmorito, Count Radicati di, 59
Martucci, Giuseppe, 81
Marxsen, Eduard, 10, 11, 12, 23, 31, 33, 38, 72
Mason, William, 20
May, Florence, 54
Mehlem, 22
Meiningen, Duke and Duchess of, 71

103

Index

Meiningen Court Orchestra, 71
Mendelssohn, Felix, 37, 61, 64
Meysenbug, von, family, 37, 39
Mozart, Wolfgang Amadeus, 11, 12, 33, 37, 38, 45, 89, 97
Mühlfeld, Richard, 90
Mürzuschlag, 74

Neue Zeitschrift für Musik, 26, 45, 46
Nottebohm, Karl, 47, 68, 80

Oldenburg, 43

Parmigiano, 82
Pohl, Carl Ferdinand, 80
Pörtschach, 67, 79

Raff, Joseph Joachim, 20
Reinicke, Carl, 22
Reinthaler, Karl Martin, 52
Reményi, Eduard, 15, 16, 17, 18, 20, 45
Rhineland, 22, 32
Richter, Hans, 72
Rösing, Frau Dr., 39, 42
Rossini, Gioacchino, 82
Rubinstein, Anton, 57, 61

Sassnitz, 66
Sayn-Wittgenstein, Princess Caroline von, 18
Schubert, Franz, 12, 47, 61, 97
Schumann family:
    Clara, 14–15, 22–3, 25–6, 28–35, 37, 42, 43, 45, 46, 52, 54, 57, 59–60, 69, 71, 78, 80–1, 92, 93
    Elise, 31
    Felix, 29, 70
    Ferdinand, 80
    Julie, 59, 70
    Marie, 31
    Robert, 12, 14–15, 22–3, 25–6, 28–34, 35, 37, 45, 48, 49, 51, 61, 64, 65, 70, 80
Sicily, 68
Siebold, Agathe von, 42, 43
Simrock, Fritz (publisher), 66, 75, 86
Singakademie, Vienna, 48, 61
Singverein, Vienna, 61, 97
Sorrows of Young Werther, The (Goethe), 36
Spies, Hermine, 72, 89, 90
Stockhausen, Julius, 34, 52, 59
Strauss, Johann (senior), 55, 67, 96
Switzerland, 34, 54

Tausch, Julius, 33
Tausig, Karl, 47–8
Thun, 78, 79, 81
Truxa, Frau, 81, 86, 96
Turgenev, Ivan, 55, 57
Tutzing, 66

Viardot, Pauline, 55
Vienna, 47ff., 61ff., 67, 72, 74, 86, 87
Völckers, Betty and Marie, 42

Wagner, Richard, 45, 46, 48, 71, 75
Wasielewski, Joseph von, 22
Weiss, Amalie, 48, 52, 59, 75
Wesendonck, Mathilde, 54
Widmann, Joseph, 54, 57, 66, 79–80, 81, 84, 85
Winsen, 12ff., 14, 17
Winsen Men's Choral Society, 13, 17, 38
Wolf, Hugo, 88

Zurich, 89